RESCUE

a daily devotional for homeschool moms

Trudie Schar
and her tribe of homeschool mom friends

Edited by Faith Stoller

Cover design by Darcy Schock

Interior design by Darcy Schock

Final edit by Melissa Romero

For all the brave mamas who are stepping out to homeschool during the pandemic of 2020.

Introduction

Not to be negative or anything, but motherhood has been the hardest thing I have ever done. Motherhood + Homeschooling completely broke me.

For some reason, I thought if I did what He called me to it would be easy. For some reason, I thought I could do it all myself. I found out that when I do what He has called me to it is not magically easy. I was surprised by this.

I've heard it said that when you are squeezed from every side you find out what is really inside a person.

Well, being a homeschool mom who is on call 24 x7 has squeezed me from every side possible. Ugly came out. I was bitter, angry, and selfish.

Homeschooling has shown me how nothing I really am.
I have seen first hand how little I know, how selfish I am, and how little control I have over how I behave.

It has been through this homeschool journey that I realized how GREAT my need for Jesus really is! I've learned I need Jesus. Every single step.

I need Him to rescue me.

If you've been homeschooling for a bit you know this to be true. If you are just beginning to homeschool, because of Covid-19, or pandemic schooling; I am sorry. This is likely going to be the hardest year of your life.

YET.

If you let it, it could also be the best year of your life.

If you choose to let **Jesus** rescue you,
it could be the best year of your life.

Homeschooling will change you if you let it.
It will grow you, if you let it. It will sanctify and bring you closer to Jesus.

Every year, even every day, we have the choice — Will we fight these things that are hard ? Or will we let God teach us through it?

If we choose — and I say we because I even though I've been doing this ten years, I still have to choose — if we choose to learn, grow, and be sanctified through this year, we will be closer to Jesus. We will still experience hard days, yet He will show up to walk beside us. The Holy Spirit will not be far away, whispering words of comfort and strengthening us.

We will become a different person when we choose to let Jesus rescue us.

I put together this devotional book for you, sweet homeschool mom.

I created it as something I wish I had had years ago. Someone to sit beside you and cheer you on. To be the friend you need to point you to Jesus. To remind you that your kids are indeed sweet. To tell you it is ok if you struggle through this year, it's ok if you learn lessons. To tell you it is ok if you cry a bit and hide in the bedroom. Someone to remind you to run to Jesus when it gets hard.

I want to make it easier for you to choose Jesus this year.

I got some of my friends together to create this gift for you. We designed the devotional to be short reads, 3-5 minute snippets, because I know you may not have tons of time. We picture you pulling this out on the week days, as you drink your coffee before homeschool begins. There are 140 devotionals in the book. Each day we point you to verses in the Bible. We added a prayer, because we know it is sometimes hard to find the words to say. Last of all, each day includes a place you can read further, for those days your kids sleep in. *Wink.*

Sweet mama, as we hand to you the words we crafted, I want you to know we are praying for you. We pray that you choose to let God teach you this year. We pray that when things get tough this devotional points you to the homeschool mom's rescue; Jesus.

 Trudie

Bravery
Trudie Schar

Good for you. You have stepped into a new year. That takes bravery, it does.

It's kind of exciting to think about what the year might hold. What fun will you have with your children? What will you learn? (You might be surprised you learn as much as them. Wink wink.)

But I wonder if you are a bit scared under that bravery.
I know I am.

But then I'm reminded of Acts 17.

And he made from one man every nation of mankind to live on all the face of the earth, having determined allotted periods and the boundaries of their dwelling place, that they should seek God, and perhaps feel their way toward him and find him. Yet he is actually not far from each one of us, for "In him we live and move and have our being." Acts 17:26-28 ESV

You were made on purpose. You were put on the Earth during this exact time period on purpose. Though God, having ALL kinds of power could homeschool your children WITHOUT you... you were put right here during this exact school year. Given your exact children. During this exact time period.

Why?
So that you would SEEK GOD. Feel your way to GOD. And FIND God.

That is why God takes us through different things. So that we would Seek, Feel, and FIND HIM.

I know you are going to find a lot of bumps in the coming year; I pray that instead of running or falling down when the bumps come that you would reach out and FIND Jesus. He is not far from any of us. In fact, He is the only way we live, move and have our being. He is not far.

God has placed you during this exact time of history,

So that you would Seek Him, Feel Him,

and Find Him. He is not far away.

Jesus, I'm on the first day of this new year. I know that there is a reason I'm here right now. There are little ones in front of me to teach and guide, and though I'm taking this one brave step I'm scared. Please calm my fears. Remind me of these verses throughout the day. Remind me that you placed me right HERE on purpose. And when the bumps come (or even when it is going smooth) help me to reach out and find You. In Jesus' name, Amen.

Further Reading: Acts 17:24-31

A Picture Perfect Homeschool
Darcy Schock

It was the first day of first grade. I was all geared up and excited to start. I had already made it through the first year. Gone were the visions of a dreamy homeschool room as seen on social media. Gone was the fear that "I can't do this." I had a new resolve to face this year. I was charged and ready to go with my realistic expectations.

In the back of my head, however, those expectations looked like three sweet calm girls around the table waiting patiently and hanging on my every word. What showed up was more like mismatched outfits, a nursing baby, and a toddler hanging off my back asking when it was HER TURN. It looked like spilled crayons, torn paper, and a lot of noise. So.Much.Noise.

"Picture perfect," I mockingly said under my breath. We were one day in and I was quickly realizing my expectations were still too high. One measly day and I was wondering if I would manage to teach them anything at all.

Later that afternoon, feeling a bit discouraged, I texted my sister-in-law (who also homeschools) describing my scenario. She replied simply:

"It was picture perfect. I could picture it perfectly."

All of the sudden, I didn't feel so alone. I felt a bit less crazy. I felt grace and understanding enter the picture. I felt hope knowing someone else could relate and has walked this path before me. It gave me a tiny step of resolve to keep going because I wasn't alone, someone understood.

While it was comforting to know that my sister-in-law could picture my struggle perfectly and sympathize well, I know someone who does an even better job. Better yet, He is available 24/7. Jesus understands our struggles even better than our closest homeschool friend. He sees our heart. He walks with us daily. He has felt the things we feel. He knows our children better than we know them. When we look to Him, not only will we find guidance, we will find understanding and comfort.

My friend, be open with other homeschool mommas. Let them in on your day and encourage each other. But above all else, look to Jesus. We will never be perfect but He is. When we let go of our idea of perfection and rest in Him to guide us, we will find the strength we need to homeschool our kids in the exact way they need. No picture perfect expectations required; just a calm assurance that the Perfect One has got this.

" For we do not have a high priest who is unable to sympathize with our weaknesses, but one who in every respect has been tempted as we are, yet without sin." Hebrews 4:15 ESV

Lord, thank you for walking this path of life before me. I pray that you would place people in my path that understand and sympathize with me on this journey. Remind me to always keep my eyes focused on You. Thank You for being the perfect One who can comfort and guide me in the exact way I need. In Jesus' name, Amen.

Further Reading: Hebrews 12:1-3

Day Three
Trudie Schar

This one is the hardest day of homeschool for me. . .

The newness has worn off. The fun start of homeschool activities have been forgotten. The work has begun. And I usually want to quit. Today. Day three.

Day three used to surprise me. But no more. It used to hit me like a head on collision. I would wake up and wonder what had hit me. But no more.

Day three no longer has that control over me, because I know it is coming.
It seems silly to even say this out loud ... but I prepare for day three.

Day one. It's exciting; I need someone to talk to. To tell someone how it went, the good, the bad, and the things we need to switch out.

Day two. It's ok. It's not quite as fun. But I'm ok. I need some time to think through if the adjustments I made worked better or need more tweaking.

Day three. I just want to stay in bed. The adrenaline has worn off. I'm ready for a long nap.

So mama, if you feel the same. . . You are not alone. Not at all. Many homeschool moms have wanted to quit on day three. You are not the only one.

Here is what to do about it. . . Just make it through day three. Day four is coming. It is better, I promise. Don't give up now. Remember WHY you are doing this. Take a moment to look at your family picture. Aren't those kids cute? Yes, I know you may not admit it. . . But they are. They are precious. You can get out of bed and meet their eager eyes with a smile.

(The thing about day three... sometimes your kids are tired too... sometimes they are over excited. Oftentimes there is a mix of both.) That is what makes you more tired. Wink

I know you know where to go for more strength. Run to Him. Plead with Him to give you strength for day three. And then just keep going. Day three doesn't last forever.

He giveth power to the faint; and to them that have no might he increaseth strength.
Isaiah 40:29 KJV

Jesus, give me strength when I am weak. I'm tired today. The bed just seems like a good place to stay. Give me the energy I need to get through day three. You are the one with the strength. Please fill me today. In Your name I pray, Amen.

Further Reading: Isaiah 40:28-31

You are Called
Jessica Heinlen

Anxiety. Fear. Doubt. All these emotions filled my mind. How can I do this? How can I homeschool when I can barely run a household and keep up with the dishes! Surely I must be out of my mind!

These were the thoughts that ran through my mind the entire summer before our first year homeschooling. Not to mention, our extended family was not on board with the idea of us pulling our kids out of the public school system.

I felt alone.

I wasn't confident in myself or my abilities for sure. I was barely hanging on as a stay-at-home mom so I really didn't know if I could do this homeschool thing on top of it.

However, the big game changer for me that I was certain of, was this....I was called. Called by God to be the mother of these six beautiful children. Called by God to be a stay-at-home mom. Called by God, the Creator of the universe, to homeschool my children. I was called!

I was Called

As I looked back on the months leading up to this, I saw how God was preparing me. In the months preceding our decision to homeschool, my prayer journal was filled with prayers asking God to help me abide in his will. Reminders that God will give me all that I need from His glorious riches in Christ Jesus and that ultimately God is in control of everything that touches my life! God was preparing my heart for what was to come even though I didn't realize it. All I needed to do was have faith.

You my dear, have been called by our creator for such a time as this. Even if you didn't expect it at all! Embrace it. Enjoy it. Rise up. And pray without ceasing.

One thing I have been reminded of over and over again is the quote, "God does not call the equipped, He equips the called!"

"All Scripture is breathed out by God and profitable for teaching, for reproof, for correction, and for training in righteousness, that the man of God may be complete, equipped for every good work."
2 Timothy 3:16-17 ESV

"All scripture is given by inspiration of God, and is profitable for doctrine, for reproof, for correction, for instruction in righteousness: That the man of God may be perfect, thoroughly furnished unto all good works."
2 Timothy 3:16-17 KJV

Lord, thank you for calling me to homeschool my child(ren). Thank you for preparing and equipping me for every good work. May you lead and guide me by your Holy Spirit to do your will and may all that I do be pleasing in your sight. In Jesus' name, Amen.

Further Reading: Hebrews 13:20-21

There is a Reason for It
Trudie Schar

I was following a truck the other day. I had places to be... but he obviously did not. He was poking along. I poked along behind him annoyed. After several miles, I finally looked at the truck closer. In the back end was some very nice furniture. It looked like a dresser and night stand. Finally, it made sense why he was crawling along the road so slowly! He was protecting the furniture in the truck bed.

It hit me though... How many times am I annoyed with my children's turtle pace? Ugh. Hopefully I keep the annoyance inside my head without them knowing it. But there have been a couple instances when I mess it up.

As I watched the truck in front of me poke along it hit me THERE is a reason for its going slow. Often ... too often with hormonal girls, there is a reason why they are poking along. They are still feeling bad about something that happened last week. Or they are worried about what someone thinks of them. Or they are concerned about ordering something. Or without a cause they are just having a rough day...

There is a reason they are going at a turtle's pace.

This truck here is a good reminder to me — stop and look at their hearts. Why are they poking around? Why are they going slowly on their work? Why can't they concentrate? Perhaps there is a reason. If there is a reason, perhaps there is something that I can help them sort out in their minds. Perhaps they can work through their feelings and be able to concentrate better.

{Really, if I'm honest with myself, I can be the same way ... I worry about similar things that my girls have on their minds. Sigh. I should take my own advice. Wink}

Go to the ant, thou sluggard; consider her ways, and be wise: Proverbs 6:6 KJV

Jesus, thank you for helping me see that sometimes there is a reason my kids are going pokey. Help me to stop and take a moment before getting annoyed with their pace. Help us figure out what is causing their distraction. If there is a way I can help them walk through their emotions, give me the words to help them sort it out. In Jesus' name, Amen.

Further Reading: Proverbs 6:6-11

Congrats On The New Job
Trudie Schar

So you've been on your new job for a week. How's it going? No, really, how is it?

Does it feel like a job? Part-time? Full-time?

There have been years where I didn't think my ability to get household things done should change. I should be able to do it all like I did during the summer. Then one year I counted how many hours I spent at "school" with the kids. It was astronomical. It really blew my mind.

No longer could I treat it as if it didn't take time. No longer could I manage to expect myself to do as much as I did when school was out. I was finally able to admit to myself that I had a JOB. One in which I clocked many hours.

Knowing that was the first step in finding a weird sort of freedom. Treating my time as though I had a job was key. I started being able to mentally let the housework go until I was "done" with my homeschool job. I stopped beating myself up for not being able to do it all. And it's odd, somehow, by accepting this as a "real job" I think I began to get more done.

Treat Homeschooling as a job.

Admit it takes time to do, and you will experience freedom.

Treat homeschooling as a job. Admit it takes time to do, and you will experience freedom.

Whatsoever thy hand findeth to do, do it with thy might; for there is no work, nor device, nor knowledge, nor wisdom, in the grave, whither thou goest.

Ecclesiastes 9:10 KJV

Jesus, it's hard to look around and realize I don't have as much time as I used to. Help me to guard my mind from beating myself up for the things I haven't had time to do lately. Help me make that transformation in my mind, this is a job that takes time. Help me to focus on homeschooling and let the rest of the to-do list go during school hours. Then once school is done for the day fill me with the energy I need for the household chores and the to-do list. Help me guard my time and energy and focus it on only the most important things. In Jesus' name, Amen.

Further Reading: Ecclesiastes 9:7-12

Clean Kitchens are Overrated
Nancy Beach

"Where there are no oxen, the manger is clean, but abundant crops come by the strength of the ox." Proverbs 14:4 ESV

My heart pounded as my doorbell rang over and over. I threw open the door and my neighbor rushed into my house.

"Buckets, we need buckets of water." There was a car on fire in front of my house. It turned out to be a minor issue. After the police left, I shut my door and looked at the house from my neighbor's eyes. We'd tossed last night's supper dishes out of the sink to fill the buckets. There were two loads of laundry on the couch waiting to be folded. Homeschool papers strewed the kitchen table.

What must she think of me?

Then I remembered my other homeschool friend's favorite verse, "Where there are no oxen, the manger is clean." (Proverbs 14:4a ESV) The homeschool translation sounds a little like this: "Where there are no children, sinks are shiny, laundry is folded, and no one is stepping on Legos in the middle of the night."

I reminded myself training these little ones God entrusted to me was more important than having a spotless house. This was a season. And this mama only had so much energy in a day. My calling today was to sit on the couch and read to my littles. It was to grade the math papers and be thankful for answer keys in the back of the book.

God is most concerned with how much I am loving Him and those around me. (Matthew 22:37-38).

Dishes eventually get done. Laundry gets folded. And just because my kitchen looked like a disaster zone today, I remembered there were plenty of moments when it didn't. It was okay today I chose to sleep the extra half hour so I would have the strength and patience to navigate the day with some degree of grace. It was okay that we went for a family walk instead of doing the dishes last night.

Now my manger is clean. My littles have grown into competent healthy adults and left home. Gone are the days of endless laundry and dishes. When I look back at how short the season of homeschooling was, (which surely didn't seem so at the time) I don't regret any love or energy I poured into them because the effects are eternal. As to my messy house? Turns out my neighbor didn't even care after all.

Thank you, Jesus, for loving me. Help me to care for myself mentally, physically, and spiritually so I can love you and those around me. Thank you for your power today to keep my priorities straight and not sweat the small stuff. Thank you that when you have called me, you will enable me. In Jesus' name, Amen.

Further Reading: Matthew 22:36-40

Perfect on Paper
Trudie Schar

The beginning of school is my favorite time. Everything is all fresh and new. The crayons are still perfect looking. The air smells of sharpened pencils. The workbook covers are still flat and close nicely. The pile of books is still neatly stacked.

So far the schedule is working perfectly (yes, I know that no one is awake yet) but still. That schedule you and I made out... of who is doing what subject when. Yes, it is still perfect. No one has gotten into a fight yet. No one is missing their supplies yet.

It's still all perfect. Perfect on paper.

Every summer as I plan who is doing what curriculum for what subjects, I put in place a routine. A schedule of sorts that tells me who is doing what when. Because then I know who needs me when. It all looks perfect on the paper.

And that is all that is perfect.

In real life it is not perfect. In real life someone has to go to the bathroom, someone has to get a drink or snack. Someone is in the middle of a subject when I'm ready to help them with their work.

Without fail, it doesn't look like it does on paper.

But it is ok. Because we are not teaching paper. We are not running an army or boot camp. We are nurturing children.

It is not about having the perfect schedule. Or house. Or homeschool. It's not even about everything running smoothly.

It is about their hearts. It is about teaching them to love learning. It is about making it fun. It is about training them to be adults. It is about pointing them to JESUS. It is about stopping and praying for someone. It is about the fist pump and high five when they get the answer right. It is about teaching them to keep going even when it is hard. It is about learning and growing so they can grow up to be the people God wants them to be.

It's not perfect because it's not paper, it's people.
Your children's hearts.

Teach me thy way, O Lord, and lead me in a plain path, because of mine enemies.
Psalm 27:11 KJV

Jesus, I would love if our homeschool day ran perfectly like my paper says it should. But I know it just won't. We are human, we are a family working together. Distractions and even needs will come up where our perfect paper gets thrown out the window. Help me be ok with that. Help me remember the point, not to be perfect on paper. But to nurture my children's hearts. Teach me Your way, O Lord. Lead me on a plain path. Show me what is important to focus on during this day. In Jesus' name, Amen.

Further Reading: Psalm 27

A Variety of Gifts
Charlotte-Anne B. Allen

"I'm going over to the library okay momma?" Growing up in a small town with the local library just on the other side of the block where we lived, I made regular trips to turn in and check out books. I loved to read, an interest I got naturally from my mother and shared with my older brother. My younger brothers, especially one of them, liked to take things apart to see how they worked. I still remember when my small transistor radio disappeared! It was years later that they confessed to having taken it apart and then being unable to put it back together again!

God has used well those early interests and abilities in each of us, after much learning and experience. He has taken those skills and molded us to better serve Him and to care for our families and loved ones.

Paul's first letter to the church in Corinth reminded early Christians that God has given each of us abilities to use in His service as we are all one in Him.

Now there are varieties of gifts, but the same Spirit. 1 Corinthians 12:4 ESV

Now there are diversities of gifts, but the same Spirit. 1 Corinthians 12:4 KJV

As homeschooling moms, one of the greatest things we can do for our child is to encourage them to live fully, to help them discover their own gifts and how God might call them to be used. This is a process as they grow and develop, and their body and brains mature.

How can we nourish our child's individuality and abilities and encourage them as they interact with others? Sometimes that can be quite a challenge!

As I homeschooled my daughter and her two cousins, those "ah-hah" moments of achievement and understanding, gaining new skills and knowledge, were so satisfying. This was especially true after laboring over difficult subjects or on those days that just didn't seem to be working as planned.

In my own homeschooling journey, I learned some very important things:

- Budding skills and interests are nourished by simple daily routines as well as community or other interests.
- Consider your child's particular interests and provide opportunities to try new things and to gain responsibility.
- Group and community projects and service affirm value and build compassion.
- Teach and encourage your child to be a part of the learning process.
- Stick with the simple and limit the number of activities.
- Quiet time to process and to think is vital to healthy growth!

Lord, thank You for the gifts and abilities you have given, including those for homeschooling moms! Help me to affirm the worth and gifts of my child. Lead me as I teach them and encourage them to use those gifts to serve You. In Your name I pray, Amen.

Further Reading: 1 Corinthians 12:4-12

I Went Out There Today
Trudie Schar

I was out and about today. And I saw people's eyes. Sad, scared, and tired. My heart hurts just looking at them.

The world seems so big to all the people and their problems. I want to write a book to fix it all. I want to say something that will fix it. Do something to help.

But I can't. First, I don't know the answer, of course. Second I don't have the time or energy. I carry this load home with me. It weighs me down. I worry and fret. How can I help a hurting world? How can I make a difference?

"The Truth is I can't.

The other truth is I'm not called to.

The truth is I can't.
The other truth is I'm not called to.

I think this is one of Satan's traps; he wants to get us so focused on the big stuff, the problems we can't fix that we quit doing what we can. When I go looking out and about too much, I miss the things that are right in front of me. Things that I can help. People that I can make a difference for.

You know who those people are right? Those are the little people right in front of you. Your children, your husband. You can make a difference in their life. Right now. Right away. Chance is pretty high you even know what they need. Chance is pretty high you even know how to help them! Pretty awesome right?

You already know how you can make a difference. You can start right away.

Trust in the Lord, and do good; so shalt thou dwell in the land, and verily thou shalt be fed.
Psalms 37:3 KJV

Trust in the Lord, and do good; dwell in the land and befriend faithfulness. Psalm 37:3 ESV

Lord Jesus, the world out there is hurting. There is a burden on my heart every time I go out and see it. I know there are things I could be doing to help. Yet, You have called me right here with my children. Please help me to see and know that they are my calling right now. Help me to not be distracted with worry or guilt for the people I see from a distance. Help me to serve the people right in front of me. Help me pour into my children, husband and people around me. Help me trust that in Your timing I may have an opportunity to help someone from out and about that I see from a distance. In Your name, Amen.

Further Reading: Psalm 37:1-6

Our Homeschool Doesn't Look Like Yours
Trudie Schar

The other day a homeschool mom told me her kids knew all the parts to a flower.

Now her kids were 5 and under. No joke.

I left those conversations discouraged, I felt inferior, I felt like a loser. I felt like I was ruining my girls. I mean we hadn't even talked about flowers, let alone their parts. Surely, I was failing!

I was so wrong. Those feelings I had of being inadequate, were all wrong.
I learned a little lesson.
I learned that my homeschool, my calling, my life, is different from hers.

God hasn't called me to be a gardener, own a greenhouse, and teach my children the art of helping things grow. (And all the 12 parts to a flower by age 3)

He hasn't called me to be a farmer's wife, know how to do chores and be strong enough to carry my 3 month old in a sling while feeding the calves. All while teaching fractions to the three kids following me around.

He hasn't called me to be a super Spanish amazing mom and teach my children two languages. (I'm still trying to teach them to obey and hear in English.)

Can I tell you a secret?

My homeschool is different from every other "Her" out there. That is how He designed it to be. And the same goes for YOU!

He has something unique for you to do. He has a special way He wants you to teach your children. A special something that only YOU and your experience can show them.

Maybe it is simply the math curriculum you use. He called you to it because someday your child is going to need decimals as an accountant and this curriculum is strong in that. Maybe you design a state notebook for your kids to log what they learn as your husband's work takes you on business trips. It could be a method you find that works for making the Bible come alive for your children. Maybe it is that you really find chores important and you teach your child the wonderful value of work. Perhaps you are a strong budgeter and pass that along to your children. Maybe you simply teach your children to READ so they can find Jesus through reading the Bible.

Whatever it is, your homeschool will look different than mine. IT IS OK!!

Not that we dare to classify or compare ourselves with some of those who are commending themselves. But when they measure themselves by one another and compare themselves with one another, they are without understanding. 2 Corinthians 10:12 ESV

Jesus, sometimes it is easy to fall into the trap of comparing. Thinking that my homeschool has to look like "Hers." Or that I'm a failure if my kids don't know everything "Her" kids know. Help me to stay away from that trap. Help me to focus on what You want my kids to learn and the special things I can teach them. Thank you for the chance to homeschool my children today. In Jesus' name, Amen.

Further Reading: 2 Corinthians 10:7-18

Do Not Worry
Jodi Leman

If you are anything like me worry is a natural part of your day and mental state. I worry the most about my kids. Are they getting the attention they need from me? Are they going to be okay if I let them ride their bike around the block? Will they have friends? Will they be able to keep up with the school tasks I have for them? Will they give their lives to Jesus one day? For me, the worry can lead to fear which can then paralyze my mental state.

But then I remember that our worry and anxiety and fear can and should be given over to God.

"Do not be anxious about anything, but in everything by prayer and supplication with thanksgiving let your requests be made known to God." Philippians 4:6 ESV

"Be careful for nothing; but in every thing by prayer and supplication with thanksgiving let your requests be made known unto God." Philippians 4:6 KJV

We are not just supposed to 'be anxious in nothing' we are also supposed to pray about all of it and be thankful for all of it as we pray for it. I have often wondered how I can be thankful for something that I am struggling so much with. I think about it like this: I can always be thankful for simply the fact that I am being drawn to God because I am choosing to pray about my struggle or worry that I have.

So, when I start to worry about my kids yet again, I try to remember to first be thankful for my kids. Each one of them is a special miracle entrusted to me and my husband by God. I believe worry and anxiety will be a constant battle for me, but I also believe that with every battle I am drawn closer to the Lord and that in turn will come out towards my kids in our days of homeschooling. I have often found that when I start my day off in the Scripture and in prayer, my attitude is so much better towards my kids.

Father God, You are mighty, You are worthy, You care. Thank you for always being there for me in my worry and my anxiety. May your light shine down on me as I raise these kids you have entrusted to me in this time. I pray that my heart can rest in You instead of constantly worrying about what might happen next. I love You Lord. In Jesus' name I pray, Amen.

Further Reading: Philippians 4

Mama is in Time-Out
Trudie Schar

I'm sure you've had to put one of your kids in time out. They are shouting, fighting. Perhaps they hit someone. Or started the food fight. Maybe they grumbled or disobeyed. Perhaps they just woke up on the wrong side of the bed and EVERYTHING is going wrong.

Time out is a good place for those types of children.

I wonder, have you thought about what time out does for a person? I see at least three benefits.

- Removes them from the situation so they can think
- Offers them time to realize what they did wrong and repent
- Gives them time to stop reacting and think about how to be proactive

Any time when you can get your children to STOP and think, is quite helpful.

Ok, ready for an odd thought?
Sometimes mamas need to put themselves in time out.

Sometimes **Mama** needs a time out.

Really! Think of all the advantages the kids get from time out. I don't know about you. . . But occasionally I need the same benefits. I need time to step away from a situation so I can think. Yeah, I need time to repent. Sigh. And most definitely I need to take a moment to step back from being reactive and think about how I can be proactive in the situation.

Yes, I need to be put in Mama's Time Out.

Maybe it's ok for my kids to see that sometimes I need time out too.

> And the Lord appointed a great fish to swallow up Jonah. And Jonah was in the belly of the fish three days and three nights. Jonah 1:17 ESV

> Now the Lord had prepared a great fish to swallow up Jonah. And Jonah was in the belly of the fish three days and three nights. Jonah 1:17 KJV

Thank You, Jesus, that time outs work for my children. Show me when I need a time out. Give me the wisdom to step back and take the time to reset. Open my eyes to where I need to repent. Show me the answers to being proactive. Give me grace to go back out and keep being the mom I need to be. In Jesus' name, Amen.

Further Reading: Jonah 1:17-2:10

Come to the Table
Brittney Morris

Our long black farm table is stained and scratched. Most days it is sticky and piled high with school-books. This table is not only where we do school, but really, it is where we do life together.

It is where we gather to have intentional family conversations. It is where we gather for family dinners. It is where we share our daily highs and lows. It has been a place for friends to share a cup of coffee. It has been a place for neighborhood kids to sit across from one another and tell jokes. And yes, it is the place where we dive deep into our studies of math and spelling, and most importantly, the word of God. There, at our old sticky table, we pray with and for each other.

To most people, this old table has seen better days and could use a good scrub, a sanding, and a new layer of finish. But to us, this old table, heavy and not easily moved, is where we bring our hearts when they, too, are heavy and not easily moved. When we are weary, we still sit around it. When we are discouraged, we still pull up a seat.

Everyday, without fail, at least once, we show up. We show up to our big ole' table and I am reminded that this table is more than our home base for school. It really is the center of our home, our home base for life.

We invite those we love to join us here…where we share our trials and our triumphs. We invite new acquaintances to join us here…where they become life-long friends. We invite Jesus to join us here…where He becomes the heartbeat of our family.

Jesus invites us to come to His table, too.

And the master said to the servant, 'Go out to the highways and hedges and compel people to come in, that my house may be filled.' Luke 14:23 ESV

And the lord said unto the servant, 'Go out into the highways and hedges, and compel them to come in, that my house may be filled.' Luke 14:23 KJV

This comes at the end of the parable Jesus tells about the great banquet. Jesus Himself is already reclining at a table as He urges those in His company to invite to the table all those who are poor, crippled, lame, and blind…"and you will be blessed…" Jesus tells them.

On the days you gather at your big, old, sticky table, when you can barely drag yourself out of bed to it in the morning, remember these words…"and you will be blessed." When we come in our brokenness to the table, bringing all that we can muster up, and we still can only bring scraps, Jesus says we will be blessed. We are the poor, crippled, lame, and blind. Jesus says come to my table anyways! He will be faithful to meet you over burnt toast, reheated coffee, Pop-Tarts, and Cheerios.

Father in heaven, I confess that my table is messy, sticky, and cluttered. But Lord, I invite You to come to our table, to be a part of our lives. Help me to show up each day with a willing heart to serve my children for Your glory. For when I do, you call me 'blessed.' In Jesus name, Amen.

Further Reading: Luke 14:1-24

Restart the Morning
Trudie Schar

Restarting the morning is a trick I've learned.

It's best employed on one of those "get up on the wrong side of the bed" types of day. When everyone is snipping at each other. Everyone is on each other's nerves. When the grey outside sneaks inside the house and everyone is feeling like Eeyore.

Just one of those days.

You've experienced one of those right?

I started a tradition that on those days we all go back to bed. Yes, you heard me right, back to bed. I yelled over the crying and fighting, "Hey, we are re-starting our day!" We head back to our rooms and hop in bed.

We start over.

We get up. We try again. Nicer this time.

We've done this enough that some of my girls have begun to call for the "Restart." They put themselves back to bed saying "I'm going to restart my day... or they ask for the whole family to do so.

It shocks our brains enough to find themselves back in bed that we get a new perspective and another try at it.

Next time it's "one of those mornings" give it a shot. It's worth a try for the hope of a better day.

And let us not grow weary of doing good, for in due season we will reap, if we do not give up.

Galatians 6:9 ESV

And let us not be weary in well doing: for in due season we shall reap, if we faint not.

Galatians 6:9 KJV

Jesus, Thank you for second chances. Please help me take advantage of a second chance to start our day. Help us as a family to recognize when we need a "restart" or "do-over" and remind us to take advantage of it. I am so thankful you extend forgiveness and mercy. In Jesus' name I pray, Amen.

Further Reading: Galatians 6:1-10

Changing Up the Way We Walk
Trudie Schar

Our garage has been bursting at the seams for a while. The previous owners had a ramp in place at the doorway to the house. It was handy but took up more room than necessary. We had talked about taking it out since we moved in. But you know how that goes, right? Sometimes house projects take longer to think about then actually doing it. 🙂

Finally a couple weeks ago it was time, the ramp came out. As we've been getting used to the new layout, missing ramp, and new steps I've seen things through different eyes.

Walking out in a different way, different direction, made me realize where I was walking, I noticed every step. I walked with thankfulness that a change has occurred.
When everything was the same, I just did the same thing over and over. I began to methodically deal with the clutter. You don't even realize how a bit of change can help.

When our homeschool days are just going on… time is flying, the clutter and busyness… sometimes we don't realize what bad habits we may have picked up. Or what clutter has been gathering. Or how we took things for granted.

Sometimes we need to change up the way we walk, so we can see things through different eyes.

Do you need to change up the way you are walking? Have you gotten into some bad habits in your homeschool? Methodically shuffling past clutter in our life, have you forgotten what is important, or not realized something has been missing?

CHANGE UP THE WAY YOU WALK.

Perhaps rearrange a room, clean off a counter, or clean your car. But maybe it's even simpler than that. Maybe it's put the instagram app in a different spot on your home screen so you have to think before opening it during school hours. In fact, maybe it's to clean up your whole home screen, so you are not met with notifications while you are doing school. Maybe it's moving that book you've been wanting to read to the family room instead of leaving it to gather dust on your nightstand. Maybe it's setting your Bible out so you remember to read it.

Who knows what it is for you. But try it. Change up the way you walk. It's amazing how different things look.

I press on toward the goal for the prize of the upward call of God in Christ Jesus.
Philippians 3:14 ESV

I press toward the mark for the prize of the high calling of God in Christ Jesus.
Philippians 3:14 KJV

Jesus, I have just been going along. Are there things that I've just methodically been doing that need to be changed up a bit? Open my eyes to things that could use a change, tweak, or be taken out of our life altogether. Help me to walk through the day a little more attentive to what's going on around me. Thank You for always being beside me and guiding me. In Jesus' name, Amen.

Further Reading Philippians 3:13-17

Build Your Wall
Tandy Sue Hogate

As a new believer, I was encouraged to read the book of Nehemiah. The first time I read it, I enjoyed the story, not fully understanding the full implications of the book.

Several years later, I found myself back in Nehemiah, this time in a Bible study setting. My oldest daughter was approaching school age, and I was excited to enroll her in the small town school where I had graduated. It was the same school where both of my parents had gotten all 12 years of education.

As we worked through the Nehemiah study, something stood out to me. The wall of the city was entirely rubble, but rather than just wait for someone to figure out what to do, each family got to work on their own section of the wall.

Working side-by-side, families concentrated on their own wall, building it stable and secure. They didn't hand off work to anyone else. Here's what God's Word says:

So we built the wall. And all the wall was joined together to half its height, for the people had a mind to work. Nehemiah 4:6 ESV

So built we the wall; and all the wall was joined together unto the half thereof: for the people had a mind to work. Nehemiah 4:6 KJV

As God often does, several circumstances started to point to homeschooling as the best option for our kids. A good friend told me that she was going to be homeschooling and asked if I was interested in learning more.

My husband and I were quickly convinced that homeschooling was what the Lord was directing for our family. It was time for us to build our wall, strengthening our family in the Lord as we educated them.

Building our wall was not always easy. Sometimes my eyes would be drawn to how others were schooling. I would compare our methods and start to question. Sometimes I was tired and just plain didn't want to build that day. But whenever I felt unqualified or unequipped, God would remind me of His purpose and give us the strength and wisdom to carry on.

God will do the same for you.

He will do the same for you.

Jesus, help us be wall builders for Your glory. Give us clarity and vision to raise our children to love You most of all. In Jesus' name, Amen.

Sweet mama, the book of Nehemiah is packed with wisdom that will encourage and equip you in all aspects of homeschooling. I highly recommend it.

Fill the Little Ones up First
Trudie Schar

A piece of advice I was given when I first started homeschooling was ... fill up the little ones first.

At first I didn't think it was a big deal. It seemed to me like they are always wanting and needing attention. But the moments that I have stopped other things and actually focused on just one little one, it has been amazing.

My kids can smell a distraction a mile away. They can tell when my mind is somewhere else. No joke. I can't tell you the number of times where I read a book half way. Physically I'm reading out loud but mentally I'm solving some other problem. It's like they can hear the "duty" in my voice beforehand. But when I become present and focused on what I'm reading it is almost like the book comes alive. Their eyes begin to shine. They become interested and excited about what will happen next.

I think something similar happened when I tried the "fill up your little ones first" idea. Yes, I tried it, but just out of duty, just to check it off the list. But doing it fully present and focused on filling them up worked.

So yes, try it. See if it works for you. But do it ONLY if you plan to be fully present. Because I'm convinced that is the key to getting them actually filled up.

Look them in the eye.

Get down at their level.

Ask them questions.

Hold them on your lap.

Spend some time with them before you head to do school with the older kids.

But do it with a focused mind.

Therefore encourage one another and build one another up, just as you are doing.

1 Thessalonians 5:11 ESV

Wherefore comfort yourselves together, and edify one another, even as also ye do.

1 Thessalonians 5:11 KJV

Jesus, sometimes it's hard to focus on my kids. Sometimes it's hard to concentrate during their stories and long winded explanations. Please help me to be focused when I'm spending time with them. Help the other things on my mind fade to the background so I can ENJOY this time hanging out with them. Thank you for this time! I pray that the little ones will feel like they are an important part of our school day. In Jesus' name, Amen.

Further Reading: 1 Thessalonians 5:11-18

Natural Play and God's Voice
Cindy Coppa

If there is one thing I would "do over" as a past homeschooling mom, it would be to give my daughter more time to explore nature on her own terms, and not with the pressure of a related composition required the following day.

We tend to think of playtime as time away from learning—a break from school. While playtime is a necessary mental break from the books, the truth is, a whole lot of learning happens when children play, especially when they play outdoors among the plants and other natural elements that God created.

During natural play, there is tacit learning—knowledge that children pick up on their own—some of which is now recognized as early STEM or STEAM. The process doesn't require direction by others, it just happens. Studies show that self-directed natural play is beneficial to a child's emotional, physical, cognitive, and spiritual health.

The hours of a homeschooling day are precious and it's easy to think that two hours in the middle of the afternoon are better spent on academics rather than playing in the dirt outside, but what is needed is balance. While academics are necessary, natural play is vital to a child's well-being. To deny nature-based experiences is to deny opportunities for spiritual growth and wholeness—for connection to the Creator of the "awesome stuff" growing or crawling outside.

Time outdoors offers God moments when your child will hear his Maker whisper things to his innermost being that Mom is not privy to. Things he will hear nowhere else. Things that cannot be taught in a classroom, not even in a homeschool creation unit. They must be experienced as a one-on-one.

So if you are anxious about "time lost" when your kids want to be out in the garden, when they want to play games with rocks and leaves, or build forts with branches in your yard or a nearby natural space, let it go. They are learning things you cannot teach them from the Creator Himself.

"But ask the beasts, and they will teach you; the birds of the heavens, and they will tell you; or the bushes of the earth, and they will teach you, and the fish of the sea will declare to you."

Job 12:7-8 ESV

"But ask now the beasts, and they shall teach thee; and the fowls of the air, and they shall tell thee; or speak to the earth, and it shall teach thee: and the fishes of the sea shall declare unto thee." Job 12:7-8 KJV

Lord, show me how and where to schedule outdoor time for my children so they can be alone with you. Speak to their hearts through the wonders of your creation and teach them the things that only you can impart. Bless them with healthy minds and bodies, and a deep connection to you and your creation that will last a lifetime. I ask In Jesus' name, Amen.

Further Reading: Job 12:7-10

Do Something You Enjoy
Trudie Schar

When was the last time you did something you enjoyed? What was it that you did? Where did you do it? How did it make you feel?

You need things to enjoy. You pour a lot out to your family. You have a full time (plus) job. You need to take a moment to do something you enjoy.

Not in a selfish way... like going out every night. Or selfish eating 3 bowls of chocolate ice cream after the kids go to bed kind of way. Not like that at all. (I talk about that in another devotional)

But in a "do something you enjoy so you come back refreshed type of thing."

Do you enjoy watching your kids playing in the pool or riding their bikes? The smiles on their faces when they get back from a bike ride or a jump on the trampoline. The giggles you hear from the backyard. It does something fun for your heart when you see your kids enjoying an activity.

Flip the story and you do something you enjoy, it excites your kids. And your husband. They love seeing you enjoy something.

Maybe it's getting lost in a book. Sitting in the sun. Or watching a Netflix series you enjoy. The key is not to be selfish about it, but to take some time today to enjoy a few moments.

Let the to-do list go for a few minutes and do something you enjoy today. Just see what happens.

Also that everyone should eat and drink and take pleasure in all his toil—this is God's gift to man. Ecclesiastes 3:13 ESV

And also that every man should eat and drink, and enjoy the good of all his labour, it is the gift of God. Ecclesiastes 3:13 KJV

Jesus, I love seeing my children enjoying a game or activity. It's hard to believe that they like seeing me enjoy something. You know how pressing things can get; it is tough to let my to-do go and do something that I just enjoy. I'm going to try it today. Help me think of an activity that can refresh, relax, and provide a bit of rest for me. Of course, help that I don't do it too long and forget that I'm really still a mom. But long enough to feel ready to go back and serve my kids. I praise you for providing rest for my soul. In Jesus' name, Amen.

Further Reading: Ecclesiastes 3:12-14

Satan's Lies
Trudie Schar

Every year Satan bombards me with a list of lies.

He says things like "You are not a real teacher."
"You are a failure."
"You are not really cut out for this job."

That ole devil tells me I'm going to ruin my kids. He tells me I'm not going to make it through another year.

But Satan is a liar. Really, he is the FATHER of Lies!

He was a murderer from the beginning, and does not stand in the truth, because there is no truth in him. When he lies, he speaks out of his own character, for he is a liar and the father of lies. John 8:44 ESV

He was a murderer from the beginning, and abode not in the truth, because there is no truth in him. When he speaketh a lie, he speaketh of his own: for he is a liar, and the father of it. John 8:44 KJV

The odd thing about Satan's list is that the things on it may be true about me sometimes. That's what makes Satan's list so confusing.

Yet, God's list about me is more true!

God gave me my children... I was their first teacher, taught them to eat, talk, play... I am a teacher. God forgives. In fact, He doesn't even remember it. He gives me a lesson and another chance.

I was made for this exact job. These exact children. This exact school year.

It is true, ALONE, I am NOT cut out for it, but with Jesus beside me I am.

What Satan says about me is true... but what God says is truer.

What **God** says about me is truer.

Satan is the father of lies.

What lie does Satan have you focused on today? What is the real truth? The truth that God says? God is ready to dispel the lies Satan wants to tell over our lives.

God gave you the children, He did... you are a teacher.

God forgives. He has a lesson to teach and another chance for you.

You were made for this exact job.

Jesus, I can't do this on my own. I NEED You to help me. I know you called me to this exact calling. I know You asked me to homeschool my kids this year. Help me. Satan is saying I'm not good enough. He's saying I'm going to mess it all up. Please help me focus on the Truth today. In Jesus' name, Amen.

Further Reading: John 8:39-47

Be Still
Toni Studer

I remember the moment when everyone's phones in church started beeping and we realized that a tornado warning was in effect in our direct area. Panic came over me as I grabbed my children and hurried into the ladies' bathroom with the rest of the moms and their young children. I remember vividly, being trapped in that bathroom at the church with only 3 of my 4 kids as I waited to see if the tornado was going to hit the church. I remember being so worried about my baby, who was in another part of the church with the nursery workers, and my husband, who was probably outside watching the storm. I remember trying to hold it all together and smile as every other lady crammed in that bathroom seemed happy and totally fine.

Have you ever felt desperate? Like life is uncertain? Like everyone else seems to have it together except for you?

God says, "Be still and know that I am God!" How amazing is that promise?! To have the creator of this huge world that we live in, whisper in times of storm, "Be still! And know that I am God."

When your house is a disaster, your child failed their math test, your youngest just wrote on the couch with a permanent marker, and your husband just called and said that he has to work late.....Be still! And know that HE IS GOD!

When you are trying to balance being a loving wife, a patient mother, a calm homeschool teacher, a joyful house keeper and everything seems to be piling up and overwhelming you....Be still! And know that HE IS GOD!

Something my husband has always told me to help put things into perspective is, "There is always someone out there who has it worse than we do!" That is so true, isn't it? Does that mean that what you are struggling with right now doesn't matter to God? Absolutely not! He is your Father! He wants to wrap His mighty arms around you and remind you to be still....and know that He is God!

"Be still, and know that I am God. I will be exalted among the nations, I will be exalted in the earth!" Psalm 46:10 ESV

Be still, and know that I am God: I will be exalted among the heathen, I will be exalted in the earth. Psalm 46:10 KJV

Heavenly Father, I pray that you will teach me to turn to you for help with everything, big or small! I praise you for your faithfulness to me when I don't make time to read my Bible or when I forget to pray. I thank you for being patient with me when I fall apart before I even think to pray and ask you for help. Please, Lord, remind me daily, to be still....to stop, get on my knees, turn to you, and always remember that you are MY God! In Jesus' name, Amen!

Further Reading: Psalm 62:5-8.

Awkward Time
Trudie Schar

As a homeschool mom I have a lot of this awkward time during which I can't get distracted. The list of "No's" is long:

> No emails, phone, or texting
>
> No laundry, dishes, or cleaning
>
> No cooking or baking
>
> No writing or women's ministry planning.
>
> No reading great books that are hard to put down.

I must sit there and stay alert enough to be able to keep my little people on task. Yet busy enough that I'm not agonizing over their every letter formed. (UGH! Mothers of kindergarteners unite) Or paying too close attention that I am tempted to help them when they should try first themselves. And doing all this without falling into daydreaming or being completely bored.

You too?

My solution for the last few months: Sudoku!!! It's not too exciting- so I can easily put it down, yet it helps me be more patient. It also distracts me just enough that sometimes they figure out the question they have before I get to them. :)

Sometimes we hold a race. We see if I can finish a puzzle before they finish their worksheet.

What have you been doing during your "waiting moments"? How do you stay focused enough? I can tell you by experience the day goes better when you find that sweet spot of balance... focused enough.

{If you don't have any of these moments in your homeschool yet... Hang on through those young ages... someday you will be able to stop watching them EVERY.SECOND.of.the.day.}

Let thine eyes look right on, and let thine eyelids look straight before thee. Proverbs 4:25 KJV

Let your eyes look directly forward, and your gaze be straight before you. Proverbs 4:25 ESV

Jesus, there is an awkward time in my day. Time in which I need to be present and attentive... but I find myself being bored. Or distracted by other things. Please help me to find that sweet spot of balance. Being Focused enough. In Jesus' name, Amen.

Further Reading: Proverbs 4:25-27

24

You and Your Kids are Unique
Cynthia Stoller

You are uniquely made in the image of God. There is just one of you made especially by God with your own personality, likes and dislikes, and your own looks. Each of your children is, also, uniquely made in the image of God with their own personality, likes and dislikes, and their own looks. We are the crowning glory of God's creation. We are created to glorify Him in this life and forever.

For we are his workmanship, created in Christ Jesus for good works, which God prepared beforehand, that we should walk in them. Ephesians 2:10 ESV

For we are his workmanship, created in Christ Jesus unto good works, which God hath before ordained that we should walk in them. Ephesians 2:10 KJV

Each of your children is special in their own way.

Each of your children is special in their own way.

This son is a walking calculator, and that daughter reads anything she can get her hands on while her little brother refuses to read unless you are sitting beside him. Rejoice in their differences, even when they frustrate you and make you want to scream! God has a different plan for each of your children and that is amazing! Encourage them to do things that interest them. Provide opportunities for them to expand their experience beyond what you, your spouse, or even their siblings are interested in. It is easier to work with what God has given us, then to try to change God's mold into our own image.

Deliberately spend time with your children individually. I like to wash and dry the dishes with a child at a time. You may like to take walks, or have something special you do with each child. Observe them. Talk to them. Get to know them, and then cheer them on for God's glory!

Father, thank you for making me in Thy image and unique in my own way. Open my eyes to the uniqueness of each of my children. Give me wisdom, Lord, to encourage them in a way that glorifies Thee! In Jesus' name, Amen.

Further Reading: Genesis 1:24-31

25

Being A Good Listener
Trudie Schar

Today, my devotional was speaking of teaching our kids to listen and obey the FIRST time. It went on to say WHY it is important for us to teach our children this.

Do you know why?

I have to admit sometimes I just want them to obey me to make it EASY on myself. I detest repeating myself over and over again. I would love it if they just plain ole obeyed the first time. But that — that is selfish.

We should be wanting to teach our kids to obey for more than just that.

This devotional went on to say that we should teach our children to be ready to listen and obey us so that they will obey God. And taking it a step further teaches them to do it the first time.

Yes, I want to teach this to my girls. I want them to know how to obey God right away. That reason for teaching them to obey is much more big picture than my selfish little reason.

Yet, then it hit me. How can I teach them that, if I'm not doing it myself? What has God been asking you to do lately? Is there something He's been wanting you to work on? Patience, the amount of yelling you've been doing, paying attention to an area you've been neglecting?

Are you obeying?

Kids won't learn to listen to God, if they don't see us listening to God.
Sigh. I have work to do today.

Jesus answered him, "If anyone loves me, he will keep my word, and my Father will love him, and we will come to him and make our home with him. John 14:23 ESV

Jesus answered and said unto him, If a man love me, he will keep my words: and my Father will love him, and we will come unto him, and make our abode with him. John 14:23 KJV

Jesus, I know You want us to teach our children to listen and obey. You see how much work it is to teach them this. Help me not grow weary in the teaching. Help me to follow through with being sure they obey when I ask them to do something. Ugh, this obey stuff isn't just for them; this is for me too. Help me to listen and obey You. Help me to be a good example of this to my children. In Jesus' name, Amen.

Further Reading: John 14:23 & 24

26

Building Up Or Tearing Down
Trudie Schar

I was furious! The house was a mess, we were trying to get to something at 10:30am, trying to pack lunch for later, gather library books, dishes yet to do, clothes all over the house, girls wearing boy shirts, no one obeying me, the list could go on.

And then I read Proverbs 14:1:

The wisest of women builds her house, but folly with her own hands tears it down. ESV

The wise woman builds her house, but with her own hands the foolish one
tears hers down. KJV

Ouch! God's Word has a way of speaking to us right where we need it most. This verse is just what I needed this morning.

I will be honest. At that moment I did not even care if my house was torn down. I wasn't thinking clearly, I was just boiling up inside.
Have you been there? Have you been at this point?
Well, I sure was, and this was the verse for Bible study today.

It is in these exact moments when I need God the most. These exact moments that I need to be careful not to tear down my house. When we are angry, annoyed, or falling apart, it is in those moments that it is so easy to say the wrong things. Things said in anger, words or even the tone of words we use. Things that we say that we can never take back. They can be forgiven, yes, but not taken back.

I don't know about you, but I spend a lot of time trying to fill my children's love tanks. And in one of these stressful moments all the love that I have built up can be torn down. In.a.moments.short.notice.

Now that I'm calm again, I ask myself; Is anything more important than my family? Is there any mess, any amount of dishes too big, that deserves me to emotionally hurt my family? Is there anything important enough to tear down my own house?

Jesus help me avoid letting any moment of stress tear down the things we've been building in our house. Don't let angry words slip across my lips and tear my children's hearts apart. Help me to continue to BUILD up the walls of my house, with love, patience, and kindness. Help me take a moment to calm down when I get to the boiling point. I'm only able to do this through Your power. Fill me with Your power today. In Jesus' name, Amen.

Further Reading: Proverbs 14:1-4

27

Safe in the Storm
Debbie Gibson

Weary Mama, do you feel the tempest raging around you? Are your mind and heart tossed here and there by that storm? Recall the story of Jonah—how he ran from God, jumped aboard a ship headed in a different direction than God had commanded him.

Do you remember the storm that came upon that ship, threatening the very lives of all aboard? What was the first thing those experienced sailors did, when that storm threatened to take their lives? They threw their cargo overboard! Indeed, they lightened their load. With a lighter load, the ship would be able to better weather the storm. Yes, the storm raged on. God had a purpose here, and he wanted Jonah's attention. But that's another story for another day.

What is weighing you down?

What can you cast overboard—at least for now—so that you can better weather the storm?

Motherhood is hard, yes. But in part, it is hard because we try to carry more than we should at one time. Let some things go. Ask our loving Father what is weighing you down unnecessarily. Then lighten your load. And trust in the One Who is our Rescue to calm the raging storm.

Humble yourselves, therefore, under the mighty hand of God so that at the proper time he may exalt you, casting all your anxieties on him, because he cares for you. Be sober-minded; be watchful. Your adversary the devil prowls around like a roaring lion, seeking someone to devour. I Peter 5:6-8 ESV

Humble yourselves therefore under the mighty hand of God, that he may exalt you in due time, casting all your care upon him; for He careth for you. Be sober, be vigilant; because your adversary the devil, as a roaring lion, walketh about, seeking whom he may devour.

1 Peter 5:6-8 KJV

Trust in the One who is our Rescue to calm the raging storm

Father, thank You that you lift the burdens and lighten the load of tired, weary mamas. Thank You that Your lovingkindness is forever, and Your promises are true. Help us to truly rely on You for wisdom in letting go of things that are weighing us down in the storms of life, that we may experience Your peace and Your joy in this difficult, but eternally rewarding, journey. You are our Safety IN the Storm. In Your Name we pray. Amen.

Read Psalm 107 to see how the Lord delivers us from all our distress.

28

Did You Eat Lunch Today?
Trudie Schar

Do you ever get so busy you forget to eat lunch? Ya, me too. Sometimes I find myself with the mid afternoon grumpies and think, wow why am I so grumpy? Then I realize that I have not had lunch.

Ugh.

There's a story where Jesus sent His disciples out to preach, heal, and minster to people. They returned excited about all that they had seen and heard and done. But they were WORN out. Read what Jesus told them

And he said unto them, Come ye yourselves apart into a desert place, and rest a while: for there were many coming and going, and they had no leisure so much as to eat. Mark 6:31 KJV

And he said to them, "Come away by yourselves to a desolate place and rest a while." For many were coming and going, and they had no leisure even to eat. Mark 6:31 ESV

Whew!! Does it sound familiar? It sure does to me!

The thing about this day in the Bible was that they TRIED to go get some rest and some food. They left that place and went by boat to a desert. (Not dessert, it's a bummer I know.) But even there... the people followed them. Doesn't that sound familiar!?! You just want to go to the bathroom alone and the people follow you!

What is amazing to me is how Jesus reacted. It says he had compassion on the crowd and stayed there and preached to them. Oh yeah, then he fed them.

Oh boy, this sounds familiar. Very familiar.

You are finally done with school for the day... you try to just go to the bathroom alone and your kids come to the door "Please mom, can you just read me a book...." please??? Before long, the evening is getting later and you pull out your two little fish for supper (cereal of course) and your 5 loaves of bread (the milk) ...

Jesus did this and he wasn't even angry about it.
What a lesson for me.

Jesus, help me be more like You today. Help me to pour out and give, even when I am tired and hungry and trying to go to the bathroom in peace. Help me to do this without the anger that sometimes wants to boil up. Help me do this freely and willingly. In Your name I pray, Amen.

Further Reading: Mark 6:30-32

29

Humble in Anxious Times
Sue Bione

Humble yourselves, therefore, under the mighty hand of God so that at the proper time he may exalt you, casting all your anxieties on him, because he cares for you. Be sober-minded; be watchful. Your adversary the devil prowls around like a roaring lion, seeking someone to devour 1 Peter 5:6-8 ESV

Humble yourselves therefore under the mighty hand of God, that he may exalt you in due time. Casting all you care upon him; for he careth for you. Be sober, be vigilant, because your adversary, the devil, as a roaring lion, walketh about, seeking whom he may devour. 1 Peter 5:6-8 KJV

"Humble yourselves…"

In times of anxiety we are directed to humble ourselves under God's mighty hand, that he may lift us up in due time. How difficult does that sound? I don't know about you but for me during anxious times it does not come to my mind first to be humble.

When I think of being humble I think of submitting, and when I am full of anxiety submitting feels like giving up, letting the other guy win; that is difficult for me to do without some pushback, that makes me feel like I've lost control. And I am a self-proclaimed, (working on it) "Control freak" with a capital C.

Control is such an illusion. We try hard to control everything in our lives so the outcomes will be more "pleasant"; the way WE want them to be, because WE think we know best. That has seldom worked in my favor. If truth be told it probably never has; and the times I believe it has, was because what I wanted was in alignment with what God wanted for me as well.

In Proverbs 11:2 we are told that "...with the humble is wisdom." God tells us to be humble when we are anxious, and that when we are humble, we have wisdom. Wisdom from Humility, that makes me view being humble in a whole new light. One of empowerment, of understanding we do not have control. God does. Of a strong woman standing with the wisdom and humility from God to overcome all things with Him.

May we all learn to view humility as a positive attribute in our lives, not one of giving up or letting the other guy win. We as humble Christlike individuals have the wisdom to understand who is in control and who can take our anxieties away. As children of God born to be Christlike, we are not in control, but we are empowered by Godly humility, Godly wisdom.

Father, I praise Your name and wish to humble myself to You in every way. Father, give me the wisdom to understand I am not in control; You are in control every second. Father, give me the wisdom to be humble during anxious times and humble myself before You. In Jesus' name Amen.

Further Reading: 1 Peter 5:1-8

30

Do You Do It For Love Or Because Of Love?
Trudie Schar

Do you homeschool because you are LOVED or so you can be LOVED?

I know some of you homeschool because of Covid-19. So I guess I need to rephrase that question. How do you go about homeschooling? Do you do it because you LOVE your kids... or because you want your kids to love YOU?

When we do it so our kids will love us, sometimes we make bad choices. We give them what they want. We may let them do a worksheet sloppy or half way. We may treat them a little too often... you know, so they give raving reviews to the onlookers. And we are feeling pretty loved.

When we do it because we LOVE, things look a little different. We are a little tougher on their sloppy worksheet, because we KNOW they can do better than that. We are a little more careful what we allow because we know we are training them to work for a boss someday. We may not give them everything they want, because we know that it's really not good for them.

We must live like we are loved.

We can only get to this place of homeschooling because we love them when we stop trying to seek love for ourselves. We must get filled up on love from Jesus. We must live like we are LOVED.

When we live loved... we aren't looking to get love through our homeschooling career. When we live loved... we can freely give love. Not the kind that always makes our kids happy, but the kind that looks at what is best for them in the long run.

The difference is transforming!

May we remember to live loved.

We love because he first loved us. 1 John 4:19 ESV

We love him, because he first loved us. 1 John 4:19 KJV

Jesus, thank You for loving me so well. Help me to rest in that love. Help me desire to teach my kids as an overflow of Your love to me. Give me grace to live loved. In Your name I pray, Amen.

Further Reading: 1 John 4:7-21

31

Do It Right Away
Trudie Schar

Think about the crusty syrup spot on your kitchen table right now. Please tell me I'm not the only one with a sticky table? Is it syrup maybe? Syrup stickies are my least favorite.

But guess what? I avoid cleaning it up. You would think that since I can't stand it so much that I would clean the syrup sticky off first thing. But no, of course not. Rather, I dread it.

I detest wiping syrup up, even more than I detest having it on there. So I put it off.

Instead of dealing with syrup stickies for five minutes I deal with it for 15 or 20. Or sometimes several hours. Why!?

It drags on. And I feel worse. And without fail that's the day one of my kids sits at the table to do school and puts her worksheet right in it.

However, when I stop and do it right away then it is gone. Gone. No more dreading. No more chance of sticky worksheets. In fact, I don't even think about it any more.

I wonder, what are you dreading doing today? Is it wiping that sticky spot off your table? Or maybe it's the laundry pile or the grading pile? Maybe it's practicing multiplication or giving that spelling test. Whatever it is for you, try doing it right away.

You will find it takes less time to finish it, than it does to dread it.
Believe me, I know from experience. Wink.

Making the best use of the time, because the days are evil. Ephesians 5:16 ESV

Jesus, help me to do those things that I've been putting off. Give me the energy to do them right away. I know dreading doing takes longer than just doing it outright, but I just fall into the trap. Help me to use my time wisely today. I praise you for these little reminders to make the most of the time. In Your name, Amen.

Further Reading: Ephesians 5:15-21

32

Who Am I?
Tara Maxheimer

We have many job titles.

Wife, mother, teacher, friend, janitor, chef, organizer, planner, the list goes on. But if we strip that all away, what do we see?

 Who are we?

Do we see that we are a child of God that has been chosen before the foundation of this world, forgiven of every sin, redeemed by His blood, and loved by the Creator of the Universe? To know who we are in Christ is the foundation of having the love, joy and peace in our life to be all that God intended us to be.

Don't let our past define our present. Live in today's moments, not yesterday's mistakes.

God is for us.

God is for us, not against us.

God has big plans for us. Why? Because we serve a big God and He only makes beauty and masterpieces. He has never been in the business of making junk. When we really know God, we know who He created us to be. Let's live in strong confidence of who we are in Christ.

He chose us in him before the foundation of the world, that we should be holy and blameless before him. Ephesians 1:4 ESV

According as he hath chosen us in him before the foundation of the world, that we should be holy and without blame before him in love. Ephesians 1:4 KJV

Dear Lord Jesus, I pray that you will help me to see who you have created me to be. Let me see myself through Your eyes. Give me the joy and confidence in Christ to do the many tasks at hand with a new perspective of who I am. Help me to strive to be more like You and not compare myself to others. Thank You for loving me and making today and the new day. I pray all this in Jesus' name, Amen.

Further Reading: Ephesians 1:3-14; Romans 8:31; Psalm 139: 13-16

33

Do Not Be Afraid. Keep On Speaking. Do Not Be Silent.
Trudie Schar

Have you read all the dangers the early Christians faced? I've been spending some time in Acts and WOW! They were in scary positions at times.

They were stoned, beaten, thrown in prison, mocked, laughed at... I'm sure I missed something. All these and more, then I read Acts 18:9-10.

And the Lord said to Paul one night in a vision, "Do not be afraid, but go on speaking and do not be silent, for I am with you, and no one will attack you to harm you, for I have many in this city who are my people." ESV

Then spake the Lord to Paul in the night by a vision, Be not afraid, but speak, and hold not thy peace: For I am with thee, and no man shall set on thee to hurt thee: for I have much people in this city. KJV

Paul hadn't had an experience like this lately... "no man will hurt you" Do you think it was hard for him to believe God's words?

What about us? We don't have people out there wanting to stone us, beat us, throw us in prison (maybe by the time you read this there will be. Sigh) But we DO have an enemy. Satan hates that we homeschool. He hates that we are teaching our children about God. He hates that we love our children. He wants to silence us.

God stands by us and says the same He said to Paul: Do not be afraid. Keep on speaking. Do not be silent.

Keep sharing Jesus with your kids. Keep pouring out to them. Do not be silent.

Jesus, help me not be afraid to teach my children about You today. Sometimes it is hard to know how to explain things of the Bible. Sometimes it's hard to know how they will react to it. Please stand by me and show me what to say and how to say it. Help me keep pointing them back to You. Help me keep pouring Truth into them. In Jesus' name, Amen.

Further Reading: Acts 19:9-10

34

God and Sticky Notes
Jodie Wolfe

I should buy stock in the sticky note industries. The only trouble is, I'd be losing any profit I'd make because I may be one of the biggest purchasers of the product.

I use sticky notes to remind myself what I need to do today, next week, next month...

If you visit my home you might find these bright colorful pieces of paper on my table, kitchen counter, on a mirror, on my calendar, in my purse, at my desk, beside my place on the sofa where I sit most nights and even in the shower where my youngest son bought me a waterproof pad of paper and pencil.

These notes were especially helpful with trying to remember everything while balancing a household, family, and homeschooling.

The older I get, you might say I tend to forget more things. People's names... What I did yesterday... What I need to do tomorrow... To compensate, I use these bits of paper. Their cheerful colors draw my attention to them.

What a reassurance that God doesn't need sticky notes to remind Himself of me or my children. He has my name written on the palms of His hands. He loves us. I take comfort in knowing He won't forget me or you.

Even these may forget, yet I will not forget you. Behold, I have engraved you on the palms of my hands. Isaiah 49:15b-16a ESV

Yea, they may forget, yet will I not forget thee. Behold, I have graven thee upon the palms of my hands. Isaiah 49:15b-16a KJV

I will not forget thee.

Behold, I have graven thee upon the palms of my hands.

Thank You, Father that You knew all about me before I was born. Each of my children are precious to You. Even though I may forget many things through the years, You promised to remember me. Thank You, for holding me and my family in the palms of Your hands. In Jesus' name, Amen.

Further Reading: Isaiah 43:1-2

35

Finding An Old To-Do List
Trudie Schar

I love finding an old to-do list. You know that one you find, when you finally clean off your desk or when you finally pick up the white thing sticking out from under a dresser. Or the one you find stuck in the pile of papers you still have to grade yet. Yeah, that list.

Often on those old lists I find things that I always still have to do. Start the Laundry. Clean up the kitchen. Stuff that has to be done over and over and over. Really, I only put those on the list to give me something to cross out! 😉 Makes it seem like I'm getting somewhere.

But no, those things aren't the reasons I love finding an old to-do list. Nope not those things! The exciting things are those that I even forgot was a big deal.

Things like, 'Clean out the closet' and turn it into a hideout, a quiet time spot for mommy. . . I see that on the list and I think 'Oh yeah! I DID used to have clothes in my closet! Now I have a beautiful little space for me and God to talk! What would I do without that?'

Things like, 'Clean the basement'. . . Now let me explain; there is clean the basement and then there is CLEAN the BASEMENT. Like really cleaning the basement. I see that on the list and I think of the long week that it took to do that. Whew! I am glad that is over!

Then I may see 'Send cookies to the neighbor' with the sick child; And I realize that the child is no longer sick, no longer in the hospital and I praise God.

I may have written, 'Take a nap'. Seeing it on my list reminds me of the many hours being awake during that time while my girls were sick. (Chance is still pretty high that they are not letting me sleep at night and I still need a nap) Maybe it is getting better now? 🙁 Well, maybe not.

The old to-do list might have 'Call dentist' written on it. Reminding me of the tooth issues one of us was having. It makes me think of that appointment; I'm thankful that it is over; thankful that again, the budget stretched enough to pay for the filling that needed done.

The old to-do list, reminds me of past places I'm glad I'm not in any longer. It reminds me of past jobs, I am glad they are finished. It reminds me of past hardships, that once again God has seen us and our friends through.

It gives me reason to look back and praise God for all He has done!

Have you found any old to-do lists lately? Are you glad to find them? What is on those old lists that you can praise God for?

And let us not grow weary of doing good, for in due season we will reap, if we do not give up.
Galatians 6:9 ESV

And let us not be weary in well doing: for in due season we shall reap, if we faint not.
Galatians 6:9 KJV

Jesus, I make to-do lists a lot. Sometimes they get done, sometimes they don't. Some of the things on my list are really not high priorities, but I'm focused on it. Give me the right perspective on it. Some of the things on my list also need to be on my prayer list. Help me hold my to-do list with the proper motivation. In Jesus' name, Amen.

Further Reading: Galatians 6:7-10

36

God Gets The Credit
Trudie Schar

I can't do this myself. I am beyond my strength. I don't know the answers.

It all looks too big. Doing the housework, doing the meals, doing the laundry. Doing the bookwork for the house, the bookwork for the business. Baking the bread. Paying the bills. Doing the shopping.

Redoing all the work that we lost when our hard drive crashed this weekend. 😦 Starting homeschool with the girls. Being a wife and friend to my hubby.

I am so overwhelmed.

I am desperate for answers.

I feel stretched to the end of my rope.

I do not know how I will get through the days ahead.

What about you?

What is on your list in life right now?

Can you do this life by yourself?

Do you feel overwhelmed?

Do you feel like you are stretched to the max?

Are you at the end of your rope?

Guess what!?

God.wants.us.RIGHT.Here.

He works in amazing ways when we feel desperate. When we feel desperate, when we don't have any answers. When we don't think we can even make it through another week, another day; we need to run to Him! We need to run to Him, and BEG Him for the answers. We need to plead for Him to get us through just one more day. Plead for Him to show us the way. Plead for Him to take over our life!

Hear, O Lord, when I cry aloud; be gracious to me and answer me! Psalm 27:7 ESV

Hear, O Lord, when I cry with my voice: have mercy also upon me, and answer me.
Psalm 27:7 KJV

And guess what happens?

He comes into our life, and takes over. When He is in control; He gets the credit for our success.

HE IS THE HERO!!

HE IS MY HERO!!

When I am doing life on my own, and life is going smoothly; it just goes. When I am desperate, and I need Him; He becomes the Hero!

At the end of the day, I look back; I realize there is no way I could have done all that myself. I realize I did not do it alone. God gets the credit for my smoother day. God gets the credit for my reactions. God gets the credit for the way it all went.

Where are you at today? Is there something that you need to turn over to God and His Son Jesus? Is there something you can't handle alone anymore? Are you desperate for answers and help?

He wants to be your hero!

Jesus, help me. I feel desperate, overwhelmed, and stretched to the max. I know you can strengthen me. I know you can fill the gaps that I can't get done. Fill me with peace. Help me to leave it all in your hands. Show me what is important and what to let go. I praise You for always being right beside me. Thank you for being the hero. In Jesus' name, Amen.

Further Reading: Psalm 27

37

How do you best connect to God?
Cheryl Kischuk

I love a good challenging question that stops me in my tracks. I'd been a Christian most of my adult life and yet I had never had that question posed to me before. How do I best connect to God? What do you mean? Doesn't He listen to my prayers and then answer me through my daily life?

I was challenged by that question at a women's conference. They listed several ways in which people feel most connected to the Creator of the universe. Activities that draw us closer to Him can be things like nature, music, academic study, activism, prayer and rituals, or worship. As I spent quiet time reflecting on how I most felt God's presence, I realized that in certain categories more than others, I felt the most freedom and peace. When our physical presence feels calm, it frees our spirit to hear and receive God's guidance, love, reassurance, and presence. When I find days and weeks go by without taking time to be in nature, listen to music, and reflect, those are the weeks that I feel the most stressed and frightened and anxious to control my surroundings.

Knowing in what environments I best connect to God can help me even with the demands of my life. I can bring my young children on a hike with me. And while I'm not completely in a silent environment when my children are with me, I can talk to God during the entire hike. I feel a peaceful presence even while shepherding young children down the wooded path or sometimes even carrying one on my back. God did not create us to do this life alone. He wants to connect, motivate, and invigorate us.

The distractions of this world pull us away from His

presence

The distractions of this world pull us away from his presence.

Years ago, that women's conference helped me realize that setting time to be connecting to the Lord in the ways that I best receive his messages is a priority. In what ways do you feel most at peace and open to hearing the revelations from God? What area of your life can you sub in more time with God? Trade in that time at the gym for a nature hike. Turn on that worship music during chores. Read that book instead of scrolling social media. Intentionally setting that daily coffee date with God will reap benefits and overflow in all areas of your life. What God date will you schedule today?

Behold, I stand at the door and knock. If anyone hears my voice and opens the door, I will come in to him and eat with him, and he with me. Revelation 3:20 ESV

Behold, I stand at the door, and knock: if any man hear my voice, and open the door, I will come in to him, and will sup with him, and he with me. Revelation 3:20 KJV

Dear God, Thank you for who you are. Thank you for modeling patience, love, and understanding. We are grateful for the continual forgiveness you possess in times we place other things before you. Thank you for resources to learn more about who You created us to be. Help me through this time learn how we can easily connect more often. Thank you for always being there for me. You are a gracious and loving Lord. In your precious name I pray, Amen.

Further Reading: Revelation 3

38

Here I Am Again
Trudie Schar

Here I am again. Stuck. No energy. Not enough time. Not sure what project to do first.

The last few days I have been going, going, going. From sunup to sundown. Doing good things. Unpacking from the family vacation, babysitting, cooking, baking bread, doing laundry. Keeping this place running. Doing good things. Three days of just that.

Did I take time with God? Yes, but I can't focus. Too much on my mind. Too many people around. Kids fighting as I read my Bible. Toddler tunes replaying in my head as I try to sleep at night. Another snack break I need to serve, as I try to balance the checking accounts. Did I mention a headache?

Oh, and an electric keyboard with preset tunes playing in the background?

Guess what? I feel lousy. I feel lazy. I feel sick. And guess what? I am the only one to blame.

I HAVE NOT TAKEN THE TIME TO TAKE.CARE.OF.MYSELF.

I run around trying to please others. I run around trying to clean this place up. I run around trying to be on the ball and prepared for everything. I run around trying to keep my girls happy. I run around doing things for my hubby. I run around all day pleasing my family.

In the end. Here I am. Am I able to help anyone? Am I able to be nice to anyone? Am I further ahead? No, No, and No.

God tells me again; just like He told me last week. Take care of yourself, Trudie. I need you to take care of yourself; so that you have strength to take care of your family.

There is a way that seems right to a man, but its end is the way to death Proverbs 16:25 ESV

There is a way that seemeth right unto a man, but the end thereof are the ways of death.
Proverbs 16:25 KJV

It seemed right to me, to keep going and going. It seemed like the right thing to do. It seemed like the Godly thing to do.

But in the end it was not. It ends in the 'death' of me. It ends in the 'death' of my energy. The 'death' of my health. And ultimately brings destruction to my family. When I am down; I can't do my job.

So, I'm off to take care of myself. Get a big drink. Smile a little at my girls. Get something healthy to eat. Maybe I could sneak a minute with my eyes shut. Hide the crazy electric piano!!!!!! 😐 I feel better already.

What do you do to take care of yourself? How do you revive and rejuvenate yourself? What do you do to protect the precious body God gave you?

When you take care of yourself, you can take better care of your family.

Jesus, Thank you for the health and energy You gave me. Help me to remember to take time to take care of myself. Remind me that it is not selfish to take time to be with You every day, or drink water, or take time to care for my body. Show me what all I should be doing— eating, exercising, resting, so that I can have the energy I need. Help me take care of myself so I can better take care of my family. In Jesus' name, Amen.

Further Reading: Proverbs 16:21-26

39

Unless Jesus
Melody Plessinger

This year will be my 11th year of homeschooling. Wow! Where has time gone?! On one hand it's hard to believe I've been homeschooling this long and on the other hand I am amazed I have made it through and continued.

I have seen many seasons of homeschooling in those years. Seasons of sickness, seasons of boredom, seasons of joy, seasons of trial, seasons of drought, seasons of growth. I tend to reflect a lot as I am looking forward. I like to examine what I've been doing and find out if it's working or find a better way if it hasn't. I like to reflect to see how far we've come, as a reminder that I can keep going. I like to reflect to see the hard things God has brought me through to remind me of His faithfulness. God is good- I stand on that. His plans are ALWAYS for my good. As I look back it propels me forward!

Homeschooling is a journey.

We set out simply to provide schooling for our children, it's as simple as that right? Yet as we all find out it is intricately fashioned to our unique family and to each child's unique God-given makeup. And further, if we allow ourselves to be moldable in the process it is a growth journey for us as moms too. We learn alongside our children and God builds character in us.

Unless Jesus

In my life lately, I have been having this resounding statement- "Unless Jesus."

This applies to my whole life, but when I look at homeschooling I see it stand out in BOLD flashing lights... UNLESS JESUS.

Unless Jesus had been my help, I would not have made it this far. If the Lord had not been my help, my soul would soon have lived in the land of silence. Psalm 94:17 ESV

Unless the Lord had been my help, my soul had almost dwelt in silence. Psalm 94:17 KJV

Dear Jesus, Thank you for who you are. Thank you for being a strong tower for your children. Thank you that you are an ever present help. Thank you for bringing me on this homeschooling journey. Thank you for always providing what I need to continue. Thank you for showing up when I needed you. Thank you for your wisdom to know how to reach my children's hearts. Thank you for your word as a guide for my days. Thank you, that I can spend time in your word with my children. Jesus, guide my steps as I continue this journey. Where I lack, show up and fill all those voids. Help me to take your hand each day and to recognize the dangers of going solo- help me to always have a reliance on you to see me through. In Jesus' name I pray Amen.

Further Reading: Psalm 94:17-22

40

I Can't Keep Anything Nice
Trudie Schar

I bought a set of nice LED candles. As I was UNPACKING them one of the girls made a ding on the side of one of them. I hadn't even got batteries in them yet.

I organized shipping supplies nicely in a box in the basement. A DAY later the packing peanuts, random boxes and packing bubbles are all spilled out and scattered around.

I have my bed all made, the clothes put away, and the floor swept. Minutes later I go back in my room to find a drawer emptied onto the floor. The culprit is walking around wearing one of my shirts as a dress.

The table is cleared, dishwasher loaded, and counters washed off. Only to find snack time is just minutes away with jelly crackers being made by little sticky hands.

. . . . . . I could keep going, really I could! It's a list of all the things I can't keep nice.

I am beginning to think maybe I should just buy things, clean things, and put away things with the expectations that they WILL BE RUINED!! If I expected it to be ruined would I be able to handle it better when I find it is so? I find myself saying "Why can't I keep anything nice?"

And today, just today, I wonder if God asks the same question of me? "Trudie, why can't you keep anything nice?"

"I gave you these beautiful children, I gave you a wonderful husband. I gave you these great friends. I gave you this calling. I gave you this talent. I gave you this LIFE."

"Trudie, Why can't you keep it nice?"

The Fact is I can not keep it nice. The Fact is I'm broken. The Fact is I CAN NOT do this. I can not do this calling. I can not do this talent. I can not be a friend. I fail at being a mom. I can't love my husband the way I should. I can not do this life. I am broken. I am tired. I am worn.

I can't keep anything nice.

Just as we want to help our children clean up, fix and not ruin the things around us; He wants the same for us. God wants to take our messes.

He wants us to wait till the whole package is opened before we ding up the side. He wants to show us His will before we try to put our brokenness into the story. He wants us to stay focused on our calling and our talents rather than strewing our whole life out into disorder by trying to accomplish things not in His will. He wants us to try to keep the 'screens' of our mind, the thoughts in our hearts clean and free of cracks.

We, well maybe I should speak for myself, I need to take Him my messes. I need to give him my broken things. Only through HIM can I become anything. Only through HIM can my messes become beautiful. Only through HIM.

My flesh and my heart may fail, but God is the strength of my heart and my portion forever.
Psalm 73:26 ESV

My flesh and my heart faileth: but God is the strength of my heart, and my portion for ever.
Psalm 73:26 KJV

So, here Lord. I give it to You. Make my mess something Beautiful. In Jesus' name, Amen.

Further Reading: Psalm 73:23-28

41

I Saw A Strange Tree
Trudie Schar

I saw an odd looking tree the other day. It looked like it was split in half. Looking closer I saw it was near an electric line. It looked like someone had been trimming back this tree to keep it away from the electric lines. The trunk and main part of the tree was on one side of the power lines and another big section of the branches was on the other side, under the power lines and fanning out over the road. No part of the tree was touching the lines. It looked like everything was all under control.

Yet, as I looked closer I noticed the tree seemed to be struggling. It didn't have many leaves on it. It looked brown compared to the other trees in the area. It looked like all the cutting it went through to avoid the power lines had taken its toll on the large tree. It tried to move out and spread itself parallel to the road, rather than filling in the area in the center near the power lines. It had spread itself too thin. And now it looked like it was dying.

At first glance it looked like everything was under control, yet it was spread too thin and becoming useless.

How many times do I spread myself too thin and become useless to those around me?

How many times does it look like everything is under control in my life? I'm nowhere near the power lines, yet I am spread too thin.

Too often. I spread myself between too many things. I get too many irons in the fire. I have too many 'yeses' on my calendar. Too many 'yeses' on my to-do list.

See here, I am the kind of gal that when she says she's going to do something, I finish it. But when I get too thin I become useless to everyone.

Do you feel yourself getting spread too thin? Do you find the stress rising and realize you have too much on your plate? Is your tree ever unhealthy because your branches are reaching out too far? Is there something you need to say no to today?

Blessed is the man who trusts in the Lord, whose trust is the Lord. He is like a tree planted by water, that sends out its roots by the stream, and does not fear when heat comes, for its leaves remain green, and is not anxious in the year of drought, for it does not cease to bear fruit." Jeremiah 17:7-8

Blessed is the man that trusteth in the Lord, and whose hope the Lord is. For he shall be as a tree planted by the waters, and that spreadeth out her roots by the river, and shall not see when heat cometh, but her leaf shall be green; and shall not be careful in the year of drought, neither shall cease from yielding fruit. Jeremiah 17:7-8 KJV

Jesus, help me to be careful about how thin I get spread out. Show me if there is something on my plate that I need to give up in order to homeschool my children like you want me to. Show me what is most important. Help me be like the tree planted by the water, with deep roots. Thank you for this picture of what it looks like to trust in You. In Jesus' name, Amen.

Further Reading: Jeremiah 17:7-8

42

The Joy of the Lord Is My Strength
Danielle Hope Poorman

One morning as our children were happily playing, a dear friend and I eagerly talked (over our favorite coffee) about the culture of our homeschools. I mentioned I was tired. She giggled in agreement.

But then, something changed in her eyes as they met mine in a moment of silence. This "tired" she spoke of went far beyond a lack of precious sleep. She was weary and worn. I smiled with deep understanding, and with a gentle hand on hers, we approached Christ together.

Yes. In the middle of the laughter, throwing of toys, and nursing an infant, we paused that morning and prayed, with the little strength we had left, that Jesus would cover us with His strength and His power to keep pressing on. But, also, that He would fill us with His overwhelming joy in the task set before us.

Dear friend, can I share something with you today? Homeschooling is hard at times. Some days you'll revel in the slow, restful pace of crafts and reading literature. Other days, you'll repeat the same mathematical concepts and vocabulary words until your head hurts. You may question your decision to homeschool.

The world compels us to work and give until we eventually have nothing left. We drain ourselves dry in the name of educating our children. "They need to know these things," we tell ourselves. In the meantime, our souls are weary, empty.

Here is the sweetest truth. When you feel empty, Jesus is there to fill you right back up again!

In the difficult times when you want to feel joyful, and you can't find the strength, remember that the Lord is your strength and your help. Approach His presence daily, and dwell in the sweet grace He offers you. His strength will carry you through the moments of chaos, and sweetly bring you into His peace.

The LORD is my strength and my shield; in him my heart trusts, and I am helped; my heart exults, and with my song I give thanks to him. Psalm 28:7 ESV

The LORD is my strength and my shield; my heart trusteth in him, and I am helped: therefore my heart greatly rejoiceth; and with my song will I praise him. Psalm 28:7 KJV

When you feel empty **Jesus** is there to fill you right back up again!

Jesus, there are days when I don't have the strength to complete my day. I am tired and weary. I know you have called me to this journey of homeschooling, and by Your strength, I can do it. Help me to find the joy in homeschooling my children each day for Your honor and glory. Help me to approach my day joyfully so that I can point my children to You. In Jesus' name, Amen.

Further Reading: 2 Corinthians 12:1-10

43

Lice
Trudie Schar

Recently a lice epidemic went through our church, private school and family.

The story goes, a couple girls had it early in the spring. Parents dealt with it, treated the affected persons hair and went on with life. They didn't tell anyone.

As time went on the lice moved on too. They infected the same family a second time (well more like continuing to live with the family). Because these families didn't deal with the lice properly the first time, washing all their clothes, bedding, treating their furniture, and bagging up toys and stuffed animals; they continued to reinfect themselves. Because they didn't tell anyone; they continued life as it had been; sleepovers, sharing brushes, going to school, hanging coats alongside others on the coat rack.

YOU KNOW THE REST OF THE STORY RIGHT?

Before long multiple families had it. Multiple people in each family had it. School was canceled. Local laundromats were quite busy. The gal at Rite Aid began to wonder as person after person came in for nit treatments.

Time, as they once knew it, had stopped for many families.

So, does this story apply to our life? Is there a little lesson that can be learned? Yes, my friends, there is!

Think with me about something else that affects each of us. Sin. Just a little bug. It could be a sin of anger, lying, gossip, bitterness, physical or emotional adultery. It could be envy, strife. It could be an idol in our life. SIN. 'Sin Lice'

There are times that God reveals to us that we have 'bugs of sin' on our head.

Suppose we hide it. Suppose we don't treat it fully, we don't wash our clothes and sheets. We continue our life as it has been. We keep being busy and we don't stop to deal with the sin. We hide from everyone around us, everyone exposed to us, that we even have a problem. Others have it, too. But no one shares their struggle with anyone else. What happens?

Just like lice, sin breeds more sin.

Grumbling around is one of our frequent "sin lice problems" we find during our homeschool day. Ugh.

I wonder if your kids have been grumbling? Has it spread to you? Or if I'm honest, maybe sometimes it starts with me and spreads to my kids. Sigh.

Do you remember what the best way to deal with this problem is? Telling someone.

Therefore, confess your sins to one another and pray for one another, that you may be healed. The prayer of a righteous person has great power as it is working. James 5:16 ESV

Confess your faults one to another, and pray one for another, that ye may be healed. The effectual fervent prayer of a righteous man availeth much. James 5:16 KJV

When you are struggling, tell someone. Tell your kids, in fact. Just getting it out in the open is the first way to stop this from spreading to others. Show your kids what you are seeing. Confess and pray with your kids.

Jesus, please help us stop the spread of sin in our homeschool. Whatever it looks like right now, grumbling, lying, sloppiness, cheating. . . Help us to confess it to each other and pray for each other. Show us how to get rid of all of the traces of sin. Thank you for giving us power over the sins we confess to you. Help us rest in that power. In Jesus' name, Amen.

Further Reading: James 5:16-18

44

The Snuggle is Real
Darcy Schock

I am that person that said, "I am never homeschooling." I couldn't wait for the day that the big yellow bus would come to carry my kids away.

God had a different plan. He gently called my heart to homeschooling. As I talked to other homeschool moms, one major benefit kept surfacing. The ability to snuggle while reading and spend a lot of time together.

This prominent blessing was exactly the reason I wanted to send them away! I am an introvert who doesn't like a lot of noise and chaos. Writing in a coffee shop all by myself, appeals to me more than the kid chaos. I admit, my heart tends to be a lot like the disciples in Mark 10:13-14:

"And they were bringing children to him that he might touch them, and the disciples rebuked them. But when Jesus saw it, he was indignant..." ESV

"And they brought young children to him, that he should touch them: and his disciples rebuked those that brought them. But when Jesus saw it, he was much displeased...." KJV

The beauty of homeschooling mirrors Jesus' heart toward children.

But if you are like me, it can also bring challenges. Some days I just don't want to be with them. They feel a little more like a burden than a blessing. I begin daydreaming about that big yellow bus as my savior.

As amazing as that sounds on the bad days, we need to always remember, we only have one savior: Jesus Christ. That yellow bus will never solve our problems. Only Jesus can. He not only models for us the way to lasting peace, but He steps in and holds our hand along the way. He will save us from our selfish desires and wrong logic. He reminds us, "let the kids come, receive them, love them!"

The longer I go down this journey and the more I look at Jesus' example, I am finding the time spent in close proximity to our children is more real and beneficial than it is hard. I want to give you permission to let them sit on your lap. All day long if need be. They are such a blessing and I think Jesus wants us to enjoy them. Today will not last forever. Tomorrow you may find yourself in a better groove. So snuggle your kids. Let them come to you. This will never be a waste of time. If it wasn't for Jesus, it isn't for us either.

We may even find we learn a lesson or two when we surrender to the snuggle.

Jesus, help me to follow your example. Give me the wisdom to drop all the expectations and things I think I should do and let my kids come to me. To welcome them onto my lap. Remind me that this time spent enjoying their presence is never a waste, but an incredible blessing. In Jesus' name, Amen.

Further reading: Mark 10:13-16, Matthew 19:13-15

45

Lord, I Need You
Trudie Schar

Do you ever just feel like crying out… "Lord I need you!"

I look around my house and there are just so many things to do. So many messes to clean up. So many projects to do. So many things that need finished.

Dishes and cleaning.

Lesson plans to prepare.

Closets to clean out.

Trips to pack for.

Laundry to do.

Bills to pay.

Pictures to back up.

I can't even figure out which way to turn first.

Friends to call and check in on.

Emails of encouragement to send.

A Grandma to write to.

A book I've been longing to read is laying on the table gathering dust.

I can't even find the space in my brain to file all my thoughts.

That Bible verse I'm still pondering that I read this morning.

The person I'm still working on forgiving.

That schedule makeover that needs to happen.

The strained relationship that needs mending.

The crazy fear of others that I'm still trying to push aside.

The conviction to be more 'present' in the everyday.

I don't know what to do first. Everything looks overwhelming.

So I run to my God.

I just throw it all at His feet. I want to hide under His wings. You too?

He will cover you with his pinions, and under his wings you will find refuge; his faithfulness is a shield and buckler. Psalm 91:4 ESV

He shall cover thee with his feathers, and under his wings shalt thou trust: his truth shall be thy shield and buckler. Psalms 91:4 KJV

Jesus, cover me. Increase my faith. Be my shield and my buckler. In Your name I pray, Amen.

Further Reading: Psalms 91:1-6

Lord, I need You

46

One Of Those Nights
Trudie Schar

It was one of those nights. You know the one where you go to bed so tired and worn out. Then you are up with the baby. Forty-five minutes later, you finally crawl back into bed, beat. Then a little later you find yourself back up, this time for two hours. Of course, this is the day the older children decide to get up at dawn; leaving you no rest. You know, right?

So today I have some tips on how to get through those kinds of nights and tips on how to get through those hard mornings.

1. Pray, pray, pray. These kinds of mornings my prayer sounds like this, "Please help me through this day!"
2. Have your time with God. Even if you don't have time!
3. It's ok to skip school on a day like today. Or do "bare minimum school" like reading and math. Skip the rest.
4. Tell your kids you are having a "Book Party," set them on the couch with books, give them a little snack, and you go take a refreshing shower or enjoy a few minutes of quietness to pray or read.
5. This is a good day to let your children watch a little Curious George or Wild Kratts. It's learning for sure.
6. Odyssey, Odyssey, Odyssey... How many episodes of Adventures in Odyssey can one family listen to in a day? Find out and give the kids some crayons and coloring books.
7. If you have a string of nights like this, call a friend or relative and ask them to babysit so you can nap. REMEMBER, Satan wants you to feel all alone! Ask for help and you defeat Satan!
8. Give yourself GRACE! You do not have to conquer the dishes, laundry and cleaning all while trying to nurse, diaper and clothe a baby. Especially if you have other children. Your goal for the day might be something like: keep everyone safe, fed, and clothed.
9. ORDER Chinese for supper. (or Pizza, or Mexican, important to just do something easy)

The steadfast love of the Lord never ceases; his mercies never come to an end; they are new every morning; great is your faithfulness. Lamentations 3:22-23 ESV

It is of the Lord's mercies that we are not consumed, because his compassions fail not. They are new every morning: great is thy faithfulness. Lamentations 3:22-23 KJV

Lord Jesus, I don't have energy for today. Help me. In Your name I pray, Amen.

Further Reading: Lamentations 3:21-26

47

Friends
Tabatha Slater

When I first began homeschooling many years ago, I joined a homeschool moms support group. I loved attending our monthly homeschool meetings, sitting in friends' homes, praying together, sharing laughter and sometimes tears with one another. Oh, those were precious times. Many of us have remained friends over the years. Our children have grown up together and have also formed lifelong friendships.

I believe God has placed in each of us a desire for deep friendships where we can be real and genuine. Even the introverted mom feels content when she meets a "kindred spirit" as Anne of Green Gables would say. We are searching for someone who can understand our unique position as mom, teacher, chauffeur and cook. We seek out friends to share what is on our heart, being transparent, and receiving not condemnation but love and acceptance.

When I look back over the years, I can see God's provision of friendships at different times and seasons in my life. I suspect that you too have had a special relationship like this now or in the past.

There is another group of moms that I have grown to love. I had to leave my introverted comfort zone by being vulnerable and in return I have received much love, support, and encouragement. We are scattered across the United States, but our friendships have become strong. We have even met up in person a few times!

May I encourage you to meet face to face with others and not just behind a screen? This is so important because God designed us to have fellowship with one another.

I can honestly say that without these friendships, I am not sure if I would have continued homeschooling. If you are feeling discouraged, or unsure if you can keep going, maybe you simply need a friend. Ask someone to meet you at a park, and let your children play together while you pray together.

Perhaps God is calling you to begin a homeschooling moms support group in your area. You do not need any credentials other than the desire to come together with other like-minded moms.

My guess is there are other moms out there looking for deep friendships too.

And let us consider how to stir up one another to love and good works, not neglecting to meet together, as is the habit of some, but encouraging one another, and all the more as you see the Day drawing near. Hebrews 10:24-25 ESV

And let us consider one another to provoke unto love and to good works: Not forsaking the assembling of ourselves together, as the manner of some is; but exhorting one another: and so much the more, as ye see the day approaching. Hebrews 10:24-25 KJV

Dear Lord, Thank you for the gift of friendship. Help me to be a good friend to those around me. I ask that you provide the right friendships for me. Help me to never forget Lord, that You are my friend too. You love me and desire what is best for me and my family. Thank you for being my friend Jesus. In your name I pray, Amen.

Further Reading: 1 Samuel 18:1-5

48

Over Planning — Under Praying
Trudie Schar

God called us to homeschool for another year. The school teacher in me started planning, buying art supplies, Googleing curriculum, setting a schedule, reading books. You know the pattern. Preparing for another great school year.

I bought a 50 state curriculum. And printed it. And bound it. And printed the student worksheets. And printed the stickers. And bought passports for each kid. And bought flash cards. (Yeah, that's a lot of ands… but I need them for effect, I promise.)

LET'S SEE.

Then a friend and I got together and planned out how we were going to do a co-op. Once a week, 11:30am to 1:00pm. We planned which days. We talked about what activities we were going to do throughout the year.

What next?

I bought a new spelling curriculum. The teacher book, the student book for the kindergartener. We bid on and won, at a benefit auction, a preschool curriculum for the 3 year old. I signed up for a one year fitness program for the kids. I printed out the books, bound all the books, watched all the exercise how-to videos, printed the workbooks and coloring books, and bought the extra fitness equipment the program required. I bought shape bean bags for exciting learning games with the little tots. I bought a silly sentences game for the older girls.

I organized the schoolroom again. I set up bins for their school supplies and bought them clipboards for their work.

You get the point, right?? My to-do list was getting smaller. I was feeling prepared.

Yes, I was ready.

And THEN.

And then, God watched.

He watched as the 50 state curriculum stressed me out. He watched as the friend we did co-op with had a huge schedule change. He watched as we floundered around trying to find new dates and new times to do co-op. The spelling curriculum for the kindergartener? Well... it.is.still.an.empty.workbook. The preschool curriculum is ready to go for this year. It did not get touched last year. Fitness program? Humm, I wonder, when does that year's subscription expire? Good thing it was cheap. I just found a new game and a new set of color bean bags on my shelf the other day. They were still not opened. Yes, you get the point. Nothing I had prepared turned out like I had planned. NOTHING.

SO HERE'S THE LESSON I LEARNED; GOD KNOWS THE FUTURE.

God knew the gal I did co-op with was going to need to adjust her schedule because of her hubby's shift change. God knew we were going to be sick half of the winter. God knew we were going to remodel and move all while trying to sell the house we were living in. God knew all of that. Only He can see it all.

So now, when God calls me to homeschool I need to ASK HIM. Ask Him, what He wants me to teach. ASK HIM what He wants me to buy. ASK HIM if He wants me to be in a co-op group.

Will I get it wrong again? Yes, probably. For now, I know He cares about our homeschool and I want Him to lead it.

Make me to know your ways, O Lord; teach me your paths. Psalm 25:4 ESV

Lord, forgive me for taking your assignment of homeschooling my girls and running with it. Forgive me for not stopping to ask You how and what to include in our school. Thank you for teaching me that you care about our homeschool. You care about our needs, you care about our curriculum. Show us this summer as we prepare for next school year. Lead us in the paths we should pursue. In Jesus' name. Amen.

Further Reading: Psalm 25:1-5

49

Self Care, It's Not What You Think
Tandy Sue Hogate

You hear it every time you turn around. You have to take care of yourself before you can take care of others.

You read recommendations like taking a bubble bath, spending an evening out with friends, or getting your hair done. It all sounds perfectly lovely, doesn't it?

These things are helpful for a moment. They can refresh you in the short term, but they won't fulfill your soul.

Homeschooling is a mission field. To lead your mission, you need to fuel correctly. This means time with our sweet Jesus.

I'm not going to tell you to simply pray and read your Bible every morning before starting school. Don't get me wrong, staying close to the Lord through prayer and reading His word is your only lifeline to a fulfilled life. But when time with Him is just part of a checklist, it is rarely effective.

A thriving Christian life involves **relationships**, with people, and with the Lord

A thriving Christian life involves relationships, with people, and with the Lord.

To refuel your soul, you need to make relationships a priority. Start a Bible study with other homeschool moms. Find a prayer partner and meet to pray every morning, even if by phone. Invite a believing neighbor to become a walking partner and focus your talks on where you see God at work as you walk.

My one tip is this. The best way you can take care of yourself and have the wisdom and energy to lead your family is to draw close to those you can walk this journey with. Wrestle with scripture, pray together, hold one another accountable, rejoice together, and love one another through the tough things that life brings your way.

Therefore encourage one another and build one another up, just as you are doing.
1 Thessalonians 5:11 ESV

Wherefore comfort yourselves together, and edify one another, even as also ye do.
1 Thessalonians 5:11 KJV

Jesus, thank you for giving us the gift of friendship with each other and with You. Please guide us in our relationships. Show us how to be an encouragement and to point to you in all we do. But mostly, help us to love you and love one another. All of our praise goes to You, In Jesus' name, Amen.

Further Reading: Have you read Elijah's story in 1 Kings? He went through an incredibly strenuous time in ministry and he was completely depleted. He had not been caring for his basic needs for months. The Lord met with him in 1 Kings 19 and helped bring Elijah back to proper health physically and spiritually. If you're pressed for time, read 1 Kings 19:4-8 and see how God provided for a completely empty Elijah.

50

Pouring Your Heart Out To a Friend
Trudie Schar

What has been hard lately? Have you been wishing you had a friend to share your hard stuff with?

So many times I've been lonely, wishing I had a friend who would understand. A friend who would see me and see what I've been dealing with. And sympathize (or is it emphasize) with me.

Some who saw it all. Someone who understood the groans. Someone to hear and acknowledge the groans in my heart.

I've looked for this person. And I have found a couple people who are close at times. My husband can be a good listener, but he likes to fix. A friend or two are amazing listeners but they have their own lives and busy days. They are not always available. I have some prayer warriors that pray beside me, but prayer warriors are busy people; they have a long list of people to pray for.

There is only one person that has the time I need from Him. His name is Jesus.

He is never too busy. He is never out to fix the issue before I've poured my heart out. His list of people is never too full. Jesus hears and he sympathizes. He understands.

When I need a friend, Jesus is always waiting right there. I can pour my heart out to Him.

Have you tried pouring your heart out to Jesus lately?

I cried unto the Lord with my voice; with my voice unto the Lord did I make my supplication.
Psalm 142:1 KJV

With my voice I cry out to the Lord; with my voice I plead for mercy to the Lord.

Psalm 142:1 ESV

Jesus, Thank You for always being available to listen to me. I've been feeling _____.

I wish that _____could change.

I need your help with _____.

_____ has been heavy on my heart.

Jesus, I pour my heart out to You, please Fill me with Your love and presence. In Your name, Amen.

Further Reading: Psalm 142:1-7

Pour your heart out to Jesus

51

Potholes In Our Homeschool
Trudie Schar

In Ohio, you know it is summer when the road construction starts again. Every summer the crews are out spending their time fixing the roads. Putting down new pavement, filling in the potholes. Getting the road ready for another batch of winter salt and cinders. (and farm manure!)

Sometimes the road is a quick fix, you see just two guys and a truck filling in potholes. Other times you see a whole crew out, completely starting over on the road. Tearing it all out and starting completely over.

Ohio road construction; it is a continuous state of re-doing. A continual state of improvement.

I've been thinking, this is how our life needs to be. A continuous state of improving. A continual state of fixing and repairing.

We all have things that need fixed.

For us, it might be our school routine. It worked smoothly until our son started middle school and needed more help studying. Just a little 'pothole' repair, a little timing adjustment.

It may be our supper making methods. Maybe we used to make supper while the little one napped and she doesn't nap anymore. A little detour needs to happen for a while, till we figure out how to get it to work again.

Our homeschool schedule, it worked until we needed to stop at grandma's each morning to help until her foot heals. We have to tear out the whole road and construct it into something that works again.

It may be our cleaning day routine; when the day you clean is always Saturday and all of a sudden you hit wedding season and there are bridal showers every Saturday morning for the next month. Something has to give for the house to get cleaned.

We will ALWAYS have things that need to be adjusted. Always need to make improvements, by filling in a couple potholes now and then.

The first step in fixing it is identifying what is not working anymore. So what is it for you today? Do you have an area that needs some road construction?

And I am sure of this, that he who began a good work in you will bring it to completion at the day of Jesus Christ. Philippians 1:6 ESV

Being confident of this very thing, that he which hath begun a good work in you will perform it until the day of Jesus Christ. Philippians 1:6 KJV

Jesus, thank you for showing me where our homeschool day needs adjustments. Teach me what is not working and how to fix it. I want our day to go smooth so that we can learn and grow as a family and as individuals. Help us to become the people You want us to be. In Your name I pray, Amen.

Further Reading: Philippians 1:3-11

52

Accept Don't Expect
Chantal Dube

As women we set heavy expectations on ourselves. I don't know when this starts, but it never seems to end. We set high expectations for our goals and dreams, we even set expectations on our children. All of this has us going in such a rush. We wake up every day with hopes about what we want to accomplish; this is especially true of a homeschool mom. But this habit sets us up for failure and leaves little room for God to work.

Perhaps homeschooling wasn't what you expected to be doing at all, and now your dreams are on hold. Maybe you're feeling insecure and unqualified in your new role. If so, then you can relate to Gideon.

It was an ordinary day for Gideon when the angel of the Lord came to him. He wasn't expecting it. But God called him out to do something that He never would have counted himself equipped to do. He called Gideon to lead the Israelites out of captivity from the Midianites. But he was afraid, ill-equipped and insecure. He was the least among the Israelites.

If you're like me, there's days that as a homeschool mom you're afraid too. You feel as though you're the least qualified and ill-equipped for your calling. But notice what God asks of Gideon?

And the Lord turned to him and said, "Go in this might of yours and save Israel from the hand of Midian; do not I send you?" Judges 6:14 ESV

And the Lord turned to him and said, "Go in this might of yours and save Israel from the hand of Midian; do not I send you?" Judges 6:14 KJV

The only thing God asks Gideon to do, is to go with the strength he had. This teaches us we need to do our part, but rely on God to do the rest. We need to lower the expectations we place on ourselves. How many times are we faced with challenges and feel as though we have to do it all on our own. Instead of struggling, remember God's not asking us to do anything alone. He's not expecting a miracle from us. He is the God of miracles but we need to give Him the space to do a miracle through us. Honestly, finishing a homeschool day, week or year is considered a miracle in our home because I'm not a teacher. I can't do it alone. As a homeschool mom you've surrendered a lot. So don't forget to surrender each day to God, give Him space to provide for you today.

Accept, but don't expect.

Accept, but don't expect.

Prayer: God, thank-you for the opportunity to homeschool my children, it's an honour and a privilege. Help me to lower my expectations and surrender my plans to you. Help me to make room for Your plans. Give me renewed strength and reliance on You to do the rest. I thank You that I'm not alone, I rest in peace knowing that you have called me and will equip me for this role. In Jesus' name, Amen.

Further Reading: Judges 6: 11-16

53

Potholes In Our Heart
Trudie Schar

A couple of days ago we talked about potholes in our homeschool.

There is another level that is more important than all that. More important than scheduling and making life run smoothly; it is our HEART issues. How are we doing at adjusting, fixing and improving our hearts?

We need to get rid of the potholes that get in our road. The little things; the impatience we have toward our children. The fear we have of what other people might think of us. The anger we are harboring toward the person who hurt us last week. The jealousy that crops up when you see your friend's new house.
These little things grow into bigger things and soon can ruin the whole road. We HAVE to deal with the potholes. We have to keep our road in good maintenance.

If we let anger go unchecked too long it turns into bitterness and hatred and we have to remake the whole road by forgiving and starting all over.

The potholes of the fear of what someone else thinks, may very quickly turn into a road all broken up. We may become a girl, all broken up not knowing who we REALLY are in Christ. Not really knowing where we ourselves are going. We may have to rebuild our road; rebuild our view of ourself, into what GOD's opinion of us really is.

We have to keep our road in good maintenance.

Some of the maintenance needs to be done every day. We need to nurture our relationship with Jesus every day. We need to spend time connected with Him in the Word and in prayer with him every day.

Sometimes we may have little potholes to fill in. An "I'm sorry" to say. A kind word to share. A prayer of repentance. A forgiving word or action.

Some things need to be done on special occasions. When the 'ice' comes or the 'snow'. In our life there may be times where we know that we are going to be around someone that has hurt us before; we may need an extra dose of 'salt' before being with them. We may need to spend extra time in prayer. We may need to spend extra time with the Bible. We may need to talk to someone. We may need to apply a little 'salt', to help protect our minds from the darts we know Satan is going to bring us.

Sometimes we may need to pull up the whole road and build a new one. I've had to do this one. When anger took over my life and had moved into bitterness and hatred. For sure that was one big construction job. It wasn't just a quick two man, one truck pothole fill in; that was the real deal. Complete road tear out and redo.

This life road construction is not always easy, it is not always fun. Yet we must do it. We need to take care of our HEARTS; For if we let the potholes of life get out of control Satan will take over our life.

Brothers, I do not consider that I have made it my own. But one thing I do: forgetting what lies behind and straining forward to what lies ahead, I press on toward the goal for the prize of the upward call of God in Christ Jesus. Philippians 3:13-14 ESV

Brethren, I count not myself to have apprehended: but this one thing I do, forgetting those things which are behind, and reaching forth unto those things which are before, I press toward the mark for the prize of the high calling of God in Christ Jesus.
Philippians 3:13-14 KJV

Jesus, it is such a comfort that You show me my heart issues. Satan is out to get me. Help me to take care of the heart issues that are threatening to take me out. Help me press on toward the goal to win the prize Christ has waiting. In Jesus' name, Amen.

Further Reading: Philippians 3:12-16

54

Four Simple Words
Stephanie H. Short

A few years ago there was a time when my son learned to ride his bicycle without the aid of training wheels for the first time. We decided we wanted to take a day trip somewhere and take our bikes with us to ride, but only if he could ride his bike without the help of training wheels. He was uncertain from the first thought of the idea, but he was also motivated to take this upcoming trip. So one afternoon my husband removed the training wheels and began the real training. I wanted photos and video, so of course, I was on the sidelines watching. As they began, my son was begging his daddy to not let go. He was terrified even though he was riding in the grass. Time and time again I heard him say not to let go. We tried to encourage him every way we could, but he just was not interested in anything more than being pushed without having to pedal.

After a couple hours, I had returned inside to start making dinner. Periodically, I would peek out the window to check on his progress, which was mostly still the same. While I was cooking, a thought occurred to me. Something my son had often requested from me at times when he had the most difficulty doing something. So once dinner was almost finished, I headed outside to round up my boys. Before we went in, I stepped out one more time. This time I was right in front of him, giving him a target. I started cheering him on as his number one cheerleader. As I did this, I turned around and started running, telling him to come catch me. Then he did it. He told his Daddy to let go, that he could do it. And just like that, he did.

I was not encouraging him like earlier with a series of "if" and "then" statements. "If you keep pedaling then you won't fall." Instead I cheered with just four simple words "You can do it!" They were nothing over the top, but they were words I knew would make him soar. He simply needed to find the confidence to know he could do it. Daddy could let go. He wasn't afraid that he would fall. Instead he was confident that he wouldn't. That is all it took. After that, it was all we could do to get him in the house and away from the bike. Of course, this is how it happens, right? Once they get pedaling, they are off and running. All based on the idea that - I can do it! I'm not sure why these specific words mean so much. All that I know is that saying them will lift up a child and make them believe. Giving them confidence from the most important person in their life.

As parents and homeschoolers, we have the job of being the encourager, to help give our children the confidence, to let our children know we believe in them, that they are capable of doing so much and should not have the fear of being let go. When we are older, we still need encouragement, to know that we can do much and should not have fear. But unlike when we are children, our encouragement comes from other places. It should come from our families and friends. The Bible tells us in 1Thessalonians 5:1 (ESV) to encourage one another and build each other up. Doing so gives us the confidence to carry-on and do the things that may seem difficult or impossible. That means for both our children and each other.

Life in this world is difficult no matter who you are. Sometimes we may not feel we have the confidence to fulfill the plans we have for educating our children. Jesus tells us to not be afraid (John 14:27 ESV). Just as Paul wrote to the Corinthians, "I have complete confidence in you" (2 Corinthians 7:15-16 ESV). We all have moments when we feel like we don't have what it takes to carry on. Or that our children will just never pick up on what we are trying to teach them. But you know what? Sometimes you just need cheerleading, those four simple words of encouragement.

My friends, your contributions to this life as a homeschooling parent are so very important, especially if those plans are working towards the Kingdom of God. We all need encouragement to continue onward. So I will gladly be your cheerleader. I know that you can do it, to be the best at whatever good thing you are doing in your child's life!

What are some moments in your life where your encouragement of your child made a difference in their learning? What are some moments in your life where someone else's encouragement made a difference for you?

Heavenly Father, Thank you for the privilege of being able to homeschool my child(ren). Show me the opportunities where I can encourage them, to give them confidence that they can do whatever task is placed before them. Give me the encouragement and confidence to be the teacher they need. Be in our presence as we learn together. In Jesus' name, Amen.

For more about encouragement, read 1 Thessalonians 5:11-19.

55

Kids Can Work?!
Trudie Schar

Have you had an increase of work on your shoulders with homeschool starting? How are you managing?

Did you know that kids can work?
It's a secret they might not want you to know. Lol.

For years I did everything myself, because you know, I didn't want to be mean, or bossy, or nagging. Maybe it was also my childhood memories of clearing the table by myself after supper that just didn't want my kids to be overwhelmed. Whatever it was, I hesitated giving my kids jobs.

But then I got desperate. I needed help!

Fast forward to today... my kids are a bit older, but they know how to work.

They each have a dishwasher section to finish, they each clear parts of the table, they clean a room of the house during cleaning day, and they have a daily zone to pick up.

They work. It hasn't hurt them. Secretly, I think they like it.

Any age from two up can help in some way. Dusting, picking up toys, all the way up to doing their own laundry. Yes, it will take some time to teach them, but you put in the hard work of teaching and training and they will be able to help in amazing ways!

Look around your house today... What have you had to put off doing because you are too busy? What have you been doing that one of your little ones can do?

Whoever works his land will have plenty of bread, but he who follows worthless pursuits lacks sense. Proverbs 12:11 ESV

He that tilleth his land shall be satisfied with bread: but he that followeth vain persons is void of understanding. Proverbs 12:11 KJV

Jesus, thank You for showing us an example of serving. Help me teach my children to follow your example. Show me how to train them to help around the house, not because I'm mean and want them to work; but so they learn to serve their families. Guide my mind as I look at my list to do and look at what I can teach my children to do. Give me patience as I teach them how to do the chore. Give me mercy and gentleness as they learn and make mistakes. I want our house to run smoothly and I want us to all share the load. Bless my efforts in this I pray. In Your name, Amen.

Further Reading: Proverbs 12:10-14

56

What is the Temperature in Your House?
Trudie Schar

What is the temperature in your home right now? Nah, don't go check the thermostat. I don't want to know the number in Fahrenheit. I want the temperature of the moods.

How has your house been heating up? Maybe anger or resentment.

Is it getting too cold? Not enough fuzzy loving, cuddling and book reading going on between your kids and you?

Maybe it's mediocre? No fun happening, just floating along lazily.

What's the temperature?

Sometimes as a homeschool mom I have had too much on my mind to sit back and think about what the temperature in our home is. I forget that a nice warm, cozy, and safe place is best for growing children.

Anger between siblings, the silent treatment between spouses, the bossing around from me, to -do lists and not enough fun... just to name a few of the reasons it might not be the right temperature in our house.

Take a step back and think for a bit; how's the temperature? Does it need some tweaking?

I find there is usually a character trait attached to the temperature in the house. Compassion, helpfulness, courtesy, patience, humility, initiative, gratefulness... and the Fruit of the Spirit...they go a long way in temperature control in our home.

But the fruit of the Spirit is love, joy, peace, patience, kindness, goodness, faithfulness, gentleness, self-control; against such things there is no law. Galatians 5:22-23 ESV

But the fruit of the Spirit is love, joy, peace, longsuffering, gentleness, goodness, faith, Meekness, temperance: against such there is no law. Galatians 5:22-23 KJV

Jesus, help me take a moment to check the temperature in our house. How has it been lately? Is our house a warm, loving environment good from growing children? Show me what is lacking. Forgive us for the times when things have gotten heated or too cold. Make it clear what steps I need to take to help get back on the right track. Thank You for caring about our family. In Jesus' name, Amen.

Further Reading: Galatians 5:14-26

57

Grace, Grace, God's Grace
Tecia Janes

You may be in a season that you have prepared for, you have felt called to homeschool and you are ready. Or you may be in a season (covid season) where you feel it's your only option. Either way, teaching your own children can be a challenge, whether it's teaching them to cook, to clean, to play Uno -by the rules- or school work.

Let me first throw out a disclaimer. I have never homeschooled my own children. But I did work for almost ten years in a private school as both a teacher and an Administrator that served a lot of home-schooled kids and their parents. The one thing I learned the most and taught the most was GRACE. The kids will not remember the workload, they will not remember the facts of every subject, but they will remember the relationships along the way. These relationships, (you) are what give them confidence, assurance that everything is going to be ok. These relationships tell them they matter and are important.

Grace

So, give them grace. Give yourself grace. The intentional time spent builds character that will last far beyond their schoolwork. Take breaks, remember to smile and incorporate one thing into your day that will make an eternal difference for you both.

Three times I pleaded with the Lord about this, that it should leave me. But he said to me, "My grace is sufficient for you, for my power is made perfect in weakness." Therefore, I will boast all the more gladly of my weaknesses, so that the power of Christ may rest upon me.   2 Corinthians 12:8-9 ESV

Lord, I am in over my head right now, but I know You are not. What the world may see as a burden, is an opportunity in Your economy. It is a way to show my child Your grace and Your love through my words and my actions. Help me to remember the grace You have shown me, so that I may allow it to flow through me, in Jesus' name, Amen.

Further Reading: Ephesians 4:7, Ephesians 2: 8-9, Hebrews 4:16, 2 Corinthians 8:7

58

He Makes the Time
Trudie Schar

Has God been laying on your heart to take on something in addition to your homeschooling? Maybe a part time job, ministry work, writing, or helping someone?

I had an experience recently that God asked me to take on a big task (putting this devotional together). I knew I didn't have extra time. Who does? Lol. I also knew I couldn't take time from my family. They needed me throughout the day.

So taking advice from a dear friend of mine I told God, "Yes, I am willing, but You need to find me time to work on it." And He did! Out of the blue I had offers to babysit, a grandmother taking them out to brunch, and the biggest shock of all, my children SLEPT in. Not just a couple minutes, no they slept in for an hour or two extra during the mornings that week.

God provided. Each time I sat down to write He showed up. The words pour out of my fingertips and on to the keyboard. The book you are holding is proof of His faithfulness to provide where He called me to pour out.

I wish I could say I trusted Him to provide like this every time He asked me to do a project.

Unfortunately, I haven't. I have stolen time from my family to follow what I thought God was calling me to. And I've hurt them more times than I can count.

This time I got it right.

Friend, be sure to get it right. God won't ask you to steal from your family to follow Him. To God your family is first. If He asks you to do something beyond your family, He will provide the resources, time, and energy you need to fulfill it.

I'm not saying your family won't have to help a little bit. I'm saying it won't ruin your family to follow His call. It won't cause tension in your marriage. If it does, it's a good sign that something needs to change.

But if anyone does not provide for his relatives, and especially for members of his household, he has denied the faith and is worse than an unbeliever. 1 Timothy 5:8 ESV

But if any provide not for his own, and specially for those of his own house, he hath denied the faith, and is worse than an infidel. 1 Timothy 5:8 KJV

Jesus, thank You for calling me to take on something outside of our family. It brings joy and excitement to serve other people. Help me be sure this doesn't take too much time from my first calling here at HOME. Show me if I get too involved and our home life starts lacking. Help me keep my family NUMBER ONE. In Jesus' Name, Amen.

Further Reading: 1 Timothy 5:7-14

59

Reminder for the Mama Who Yelled Today
Ashley Moore

I sent them all scrambling from my shouts to leave the table. I was done. I couldn't take another second of their bickering and disobedience. I did exactly what I said I would never do — again. I screamed for them all to get up and leave my sight. As everything settled, I cringed with embarrassment in how I had responded to my children.

Yes, their behavior was wrong, but my heart was broken over my response to their wrongdoings. Conviction from the Holy Spirit led me straight to my knees asking God and my children to please overlook Mama's offenses.

Is it as easy for you as it is for me to make accomplishing the school to-do list more important than modeling good sense to our children? It is often our natural bent as mothers to desire finished tasks, but therein lies a problem when this is our constant driving force. All too quickly we make behavior modification our focus. We sometimes recklessly yell or demand compliance rather than giving God room to use disruptions to teach biblical principles to our children.

The moments will be numerous that we will let our kids down. Let us remember that God can use these moments, and redeem them for his glory. Fix your thoughts on the scriptures.

Good sense makes one slow to anger, and it is his glory to overlook an offense.
Proverbs 19:11 ESV

Mamas let us use our good sense and train ourselves to be slow to anger, but let's also allow our shortcomings to be reinforcing moments that show our own need to have our offenses overlooked. In doing so I believe our children will file away a much more important lesson than the task at hand. Instead, we will all walk away equipped with a little more good sense that glorifies God.

Dear Lord, thank you for being slow to anger. Thank you, that your grace is endless and available to me when I respond in a less than honoring way to my children. God forgive me. Please use these humbling moments as opportunities to teach them even more important lessons, like how to overlook the wrongs of others. Thank you, that you redeem all things for your glory. Please allow my weaknesses to point them back to your unfailing love. In Jesus' name, Amen.

Further Reading: Proverbs 19

60

The Gift of Permission
Trudie Schar

How is it really going? Do you need a minute to yourself? Do you need a minute to catch up on some laundry dishes or grading? Or you are caught up and you need a minute to sit out in the sun and read a book?

Or maybe you aren't caught up and you STILL need that minute to rest?

I want to give you a gift that an older homeschool mama gave me one day. Ready?
It is the gift of permission. Permission to accept help.

You are allowed to order pizza.

You are allowed to use paper plates.

You are allowed to hire a house cleaner.

It is ok to leave the laundry unfolded for a week ... (or as my friend said several years worth of weeks 😊)

This gift of permission helped me make it through the first few years of homeschool and the years of having babies and toddlers. This grace was just what I needed. Nowadays I still need to give myself permission, it just looks different as my kids are now old enough to help me with some of these chores.

Friend, you can ask for help. You can order help. It is not wimpy of you. Homeschooling is a JOB. You know motherhood is a job, but homeschooling increases the workload.

Give yourself permission. Don't feel like you must do it all yourself. And don't let Satan heap guilt on you because you can't do it all.

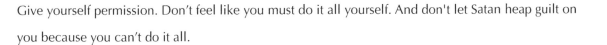

give yourself permission

Let us then with confidence draw near to the throne of grace, that we may receive mercy and find grace to help in time of need. Hebrews 4:16 ESV

Let us therefore come boldly unto the throne of grace, that we may obtain mercy, and find grace to help in time of need. Hebrews 4:16 KJV

Jesus, thank You that I have help available. I can order pizza, use tools to help, use paper plates, take shortcuts to help me through this season. Help me to take advantage of these opportunities when I'm overwhelmed. Yet, help me not get lazy, over use, or misuse these things meant to help me out. Show me the balance that is right for our family. Help me not be too proud to ask for help. In Jesus' name, Amen.

Further Reading: Hebrews 4:-16

61

The Curriculum Trap
Trudie Schar

When I first started homeschooling you could easily find me falling into the curriculum trap.

This is how it would happen. I would be talking to a friend and they would tell me an AWESOME book or program they were using. I left the conversation discontent. Questioning the curriculum I was using and worried I was missing something. There would be a hole in my kids' education.

I would go home and look up the curriculum. I spent hours researching it, hours trying to figure out if we had the money. I would have spent hours picturing how perfect it would be for us. And sometimes I may have even ordered it.

Next week, it would be a different book. Different program. Different curriculum. And I would travel down the same discontented path.

I ran ragged trying to keep up with everyone and everything. There were good meaning people out there, other homeschoolers, who would share what they thought the greatest curriculum was. And I just had to check it out!
When I look back at all the hours I spent researching the new curriculum it makes me blush. I wasted so much time.

Especially when what we had was working.

As I had more children entering school the things we were doing previously stopped working. So I went in search of a new curriculum. But this time I was searching because we needed something — not because someone else thought we needed something.

The search looks differently when you actually need to search. The search is not a meaningless waste of time.

Homeschool mama, don't get caught up in the curriculum trap. If what you have is working for you then don't get distracted. If your friend has a different curriculum than you, be happy for her, listen well to her, but don't get distracted by thinking you must try it out for yourself.

Don't get caught in the curriculum trap.

But let each one test his own work, and then his reason to boast will be in himself alone and not in his neighbor. Galatians 6:4 ESV

But let every man prove his own work, and then shall he have rejoicing in himself alone, and not in another. Galatians 6:4 KJV

Jesus, help me keep my eyes on my own homeschool. Prevent me from getting distracted by someone else's curriculum. When I do hear of something new, show me if I need to check it out. If not, help me be content with what I have. Thank You for guiding me to the curriculum that fits our family's needs. In Jesus' name, Amen.

Further Reading: Galatians 6:1-10

62

The Father Who Forgives the Daughter Who Forgets
Angel Lambert

I read in Your Word how I'd done something wrong.

I prayed and You washed my soul clean with Your blood.

You gave me the promise of hope now restored.

You poured Your grace into my heart like a flood.

I needed a getaway, time to reflect,

I lifted my eyes to the Savior above.

You shone on my heart with the heat of the sun;

You blew a cool breeze and I knew it as love.

I know that no matter the sins I have done,

I still am the daughter You love and adore.

You've given me permanence, love, peace, and joy.

You're family now; my heart wanders no more.

The Lord is my shepherd, my rock, and my shield.

The Lord shines his love on my sore, bitter soul.

The Lord is the Father who keeps me for good.

I will be his daughter, forgiven and whole.

When you have been wandering, sinful, heartsick,

The Lord brings you back with words gentle, to soothe.

You are never condemned to your last hurtful thought.

The Lord is your fortress, and he does not move.

A son honors his father, and a servant his master. If then I am a father, where is my honor? And if I am a master, where is my fear? says the Lord of hosts to you, O priests, who despise my name. But you say, 'How have we despised your name? By offering polluted food upon my altar. But you say, 'How have we polluted you?' By saying that the Lord's table may be despised. Malachi 1:6-7 (ESV)

A son honoureth his father, and a servant his master: if then I be a father, where is mine honour? and if I be a master, where is my fear? saith the Lord of hosts unto you, O priests, that despise my name. And ye say, Wherein have we despised thy name? Ye offer polluted bread upon mine altar; and ye say, Wherein have we polluted thee? In that ye say, The table of the Lord is contemptible. Malachi 1:6-7 (KJV)

You, The Lord, will be feared, and You, The Lord, will be honored. If I am not honoring and fearing, You will make it so that I am, not because You are harsh and unloving, but because You are holy, worthy, deserving. The weight of confession has been heavy on my heart lately, and I am confessing that in my parenting and homeschool, I have not brought my best lamb before You as I should. I have not taught my children what confession and restoration look like. Even though it causes temporary mourning and isolation, the results are mercy, grace, and love. You will forgive. You will restore. You will help me teach and lead my children to you. Honor and fear- these are The Lord's. When I offer them to You, my children become the fruit of my labor. Thank You for this gift. In Jesus' holy, honorable, fearful name, Amen.

Further Reading: Malachi 1:6-10 and Zechariah 12:10-14.

63

Self-Control Walls
Trudie Schar

Do you ever get angry? Do you ever let your raw feelings show through?

One of my girls was very angry. Very! I sent her to her room hoping she would cool down and be able to be reasoned with. Nope. This time it didn't work. I left her in there and prayed for God to show me what to say to her.

I picked up one of my Bible Verse Books and looked up anger, self-control.
This verse really stuck out to me.

He that hath no rule over his own spirit is like a city that is broken down, and without walls.
Proverbs 25:28 KJV

A man without self-control is like a city broken into and left without walls.
Proverbs 25:28 ESV

What does that verse mean to you? What does it say losing self control is like?
Like a city with their walls broken through. So when we let anger, hatred, wrath, anything that takes over control of our emotions, when we let those feelings take over, we are as a city with the walls torn down.
Here is an important question: What happens to a city with their walls down?
THE ENEMY GETS IN.

Who is the enemy of our city??

When I am angry and my "self-control walls" are broken down, SATAN, my enemy, can get right into my heart!

I'm not sure about you, but that is a scary thought! I do NOT want to leave my heart open even one crack. Let alone, leave all my walls down, giving him perfect access.

Wow! What a reminder of why we need to have self-control!

Jesus, wow, I never realized how important it was to have self-control. Forgive me when I've let anger, hatred, impatience, wrath. . . really any feeling take over my emotions. Help me make an active effort to fight the feelings that leave me vulnerable to Satan. Help me sort through the feelings and take control of them before my walls get torn down giving Satan access to my heart. Teach me how to teach this to my children. Thank You for this picture story that we can learn from. In Jesus' name, Amen.

Further Reading: Proverbs 25:24-28

64

Beauty for Ashes
Barb Schwind

One thing that we have all learned during this time of COVID-19 is that many things in life are not under our control.

A worldwide pandemic has brought many types of stresses into people's lives - health concerns, financial concerns, job concerns, schooling concerns, disruption of church services and other events, and social isolation. Information is constantly changing. It is sometimes difficult to discern truth. How is this affecting my children?

Surely this is a question on our hearts.

I don't know how all of this will play out, but I do know this: God can bring beauty for ashes even in heartbreaking circumstances when life has spun totally out of control.

beauty for ashes

Our family experienced this in 1996 when our beautiful daughter, Amy, was diagnosed with AML. After spending many months at St. Jude in Memphis undergoing transplant, Amy died at home in 1997 at the age of 12.

It was difficult for both our sons when Amy died. They both loved their sister and prayed for healing. Andrew is quiet about the experience. How we appreciate his willingness to donate bone marrow and stem cells to give Amy another 16 months of life! Jon dealt with Amy's death by participating in the Memphis to Peoria Run for St. Jude.

Sometimes God provides a silver lining in even the darkest storm clouds in our lives. Jon met his lovely wife, Jessi, on the St. Jude Run. Jessi encouraged Jon to serve Jesus. They became parents of our 4 beautiful grandchildren, including one who was born 19 years to the day that Amy died.

I am thankful we serve a God that can bring beauty for ashes!

To grant to those who mourn in Zion - to give them a beautiful headdress instead of ashes, the oil of gladness instead of mourning, the garment of praise instead of a faint spirit; that they may be called oaks of righteousness, the planting of the Lord, that he may be glorified.
Isaiah 61:3 ESV

To appoint unto those who mourn in Zion, to give unto them beauty for ashes, the oil of joy for mourning, the garment of praise for the spirit of heaviness, that they might be called trees of righteousness, the planting of the Lord, that he might be glorified. Isaiah 61:3 KJV

Dear Lord, sometimes life spins totally out of control. Help us to trust that You are still in control. Thank you for bringing something good even out of our deepest heartaches. We know you love and care for our children and shelter them throughout the storms of life. In Jesus' name. Amen.

Further Reading: Isaiah 61

65

So The Mess Doesn't Get Any Bigger
Trudie Schar

I used to just go with the flow. Clean up as I could. Now I'm getting wiser. (Why didn't someone tell me this?)

I would add a picture of this concept in action. . . But this is a book without pictures. So just imagine with me for a moment. My youngest is laying on the kitchen floor... under her, is a pile of flour. She has created a "snow angel" in the flour. The thing you don't see in the picture is that I didn't clean it up right away. I was in the middle of school with the kids and thought... hey at least she is playing nice and left it. You know how that went right? In a matter of seconds flour was EVERYWHERE.

And I just wonder, what would have happened if I would have cleaned it up right away? Or better yet, if I would have stopped her the moment I heard the sound of the ingredient drawer opening. Yes, she wouldn't have been entertained for those 5 minutes. However, I would not have a 15 minute mess to clean up.

How easy is it to clean up the mud boots and coats as the kids come in from a muddle puddle party, rather than letting them spread it all over the house first? How long does it take to mop up the spilled lemonade the right way the first time rather than waiting till people step in it and spread it around? What about the games that the kids drag out?

I could list hundreds of things just like that. What am I learning from all this?

DO IT RIGHT AWAY. THE MESS DOESN'T GET AS BIG.

Here is the thing: God is teaching me this lesson applies the same with life issues. If we need to tell someone we are sorry; do it right away. We need to tell someone we can't help them for the day, because we have prior commitments; do it right away. We need to forgive someone; do it right away.

We tell someone we will pray for them; do it right away. We need to talk out our child's actions with them; do it right away. We feel God's spirit telling us to text someone; do it right away.

Just like the messes at my house, things do not always get easier with time. Some things get easier with time — Usually messes are not in that category. Putting off things we dread, putting off things we struggle with, putting off doing what God has asked us to; does not make it easier. In a lot of ways it just drags the mess around the house.

Just like the flour angels.

I wonder, is there anything that you are putting off today? Do it right away. Before the mess gets any bigger.

> Go to the ant, O sluggard; consider her ways, and be wise. Proverbs 6:6 ESV

> Go to the ant, thou sluggard; consider her ways, and be wise: Proverbs 6:6 KJV

Lord, help us stop avoiding our messes. The physical messes: dishes, toys and baking powder and more importantly the spiritual messes: apologizing, forgiving and telling the truth. Give us strength to deal with both messes as quickly as we can to avoid them from getting bigger. In Jesus' name, Amen.

Further Reading: Proverbs 6:1-8

66

The Homeschool Mama's Christmas
Trudie Schar

The life of a mom is hard, busy, and sleepless. The life of a mom is not her own. This Christmas finds moms everywhere planning, shopping, wrapping, baking, cooking, cleaning. . . the to-do list goes on forever. After Christmas will find moms everywhere, cleaning again, doing dishes, and taking out the trash.

Even Christmas Day is not a day off for mom. Christmas Day finds her preparing meals, presenting gifts, changing diapers, dressing children and preparing for get togethers. Then at the get-together she finds herself in a quiet room trying to get the baby to sleep in the odd surroundings.

A Mom's Christmas isn't about herself.
A Mom's life can't be about herself. Or can it?

We have to make a choice. Everyday. Everyday we need to give up ourselves. I will speak for myself, it is HARD to choose the right thing. And sometimes when I do all those things; I do them only because I HAVE to.

doing it **grudgingly** is just as wrong as not doing it at all

Doing it grudgingly is just as wrong as not doing it at all.

The people in our life can tell. They can tell what we are choosing. Maybe even better than we can.

They can read if our actions are because we have to or because we want to.

They can tell if our actions are done grudgingly or done freely.

They can tell if our actions are for them or for our own sake.

They can tell if we are having fun or faking it.

They can tell if we are choosing love.

Christmas is all about Jesus coming to earth. He is leaving Heaven. He is coming down here to save us. He is giving up himself for our sake. He is giving up himself freely. Not grudgingly, not holding back, not grumbling. All in Love.

May we, this Christmas, do the same for our husbands, and for our children.

Give willing, freely, without grudging. Without grumbling

Give with love.

All with Love.

> Love one another with brotherly affection. Outdo one another in showing honor.
> Romans 12:10 ESV

> Be kindly affectioned one to another with brotherly love; in honour preferring one another
> Romans 12:10 KJV

Jesus, help me to give to my children, husband, and neighbors in love this Christmas. Take away my selfishness. Catch me when I am going about serving grudgingly. Stop me. Help me to remember how YOU came down and gave Your everything for me. Thank you for that Jesus. In Your name I pray, Amen.

Further Reading: Romans 12:9-1

Homeschooling is Sanctification
Kira Jahn

"Sanctification is the process by which God's holy spirit transforms believers' thoughts, motives, and behavior to conform to the holiness and purity of Christ himself" -R.C. Sproul

When we realize that the discipleship of our children is the means the Lord is using to shape us more into the image of Christ, we can better understand that homeschooling is not just to teach our children to read and write - but to have an eternal focus for both our children and ourselves.

This eternal view should turn our hearts towards our children and the state of their souls. Viewing our homeschool through a biblical lens is where God uses our schedules, the lessons, our children, and each of their personalities and sins as a big piece of sandpaper in our lives. This is God's sanctifying work. He causes us to die to ourselves for the sake of our children in order to obey his command to train them in righteousness.

Often God's sanding begins before we even get out of bed in the morning - an opportunity presents itself to train the heart of my child. As the day goes on, it's us wanting to be finished with math by 11am but the new concept being introduced is challenging, causing one child to struggle. All of this is sanding away our self-imposed timelines and expectations for the day. The sanding hurts; it's slow and tedious and in the day to day it's barely noticeable. Yet, as we look back on the month or previous school years, we see the faint smoothing of the rough edges of our life being transformed by the hand of God.

For it is God who works in you, both to will and to work for his good pleasure.
Philippians 2:13 ESV

For it is God which worketh in you both to will and to do of his good pleasure.
Philippians 2:13 KJV

We are only able to homeschool and disciple our children correctly because of God working in and through us. It is God's grace alone that guarantees anything "good" coming from our efforts. So, if you're just beginning homeschooling or have been doing it for years, continue to trust in the Lord that he is working this all out for our good and his glory!

Trust that He is working this all out for our **good** and his **glory**

Dear Heavenly Father, we come before you and thank you for your son Jesus Christ and what he accomplished on our behalf. We humble ourselves to your grace that it would be all that we rely on as we disciple our children. May the joys and trials of our days bring us closer to you and that we would know, love, and trust you more through them. Please use our homeschool to sanctify our entire family. Allow my children to see you working in my heart as I humbly walk in repentance and faith before them; And please give them the gifts of repentance and faith too. May God be glorified in our homeschooling. In Jesus' name, Amen.

For further study on sanctification read: Philippians 1:6 & Hebrews 13:20-21

68

The Benefits of a Chore
Trudie Schar

The other day one of my girls was doing her daily dishwasher emptying job and said something profound.

"Mom, thanks for having us do work. You are teaching us to work so that we know how to do this when we grow up. I like that we work every day."

I was a bit stunned.

She went on to say how she sees other moms doing everything in the house and that they just seem so tired. She feels bad for the kids because they don't know how to empty the dishwasher or do their own laundry.

I was still a bit stunned.

Sometimes I feel bad for making my kids do so much work. But this. This was encouraging.

Sometimes I feel like teaching them to do chores is just for me. To help me with the workload. But as I thought about what she said, I realized chores are just as much for their sake as it is for me. Maybe even more so!

Learning to do chores teaches them:
- They are needed as a part of the family.
- To do the tasks so they can do it when they start their own home.
- There is a satisfaction that comes when a job is completed.

It gives them little chances to learn about procrastination and the value of doing it right away. Chances to mess up and learn the value of doing a job well. It teaches these BIG life lessons... on something little that doesn't impact their big picture life or career. Training in small things to be ready for big things. Maybe even big things God has for them to do.

How are chores going at your house? Do you feel guilty giving your children work to do? Don't feel guilty, my friend. You bless your children when you teach them to do chores.

"One who is faithful in a very little is also faithful in much, and one who is dishonest in a very little is also dishonest in much. Luke 16:10 ESV

He that is faithful in that which is least is faithful also in much: and he that is unjust in the least is unjust also in much. Luke 16:10 KJV

Jesus, help me not to view chores as something my kids can do for me, but also what they can do for them. Help me remember all the benefits that learning to work does. Show me how to teach them to do their chores well, complete, and with a good attitude. Help me learn how to do my chores with a good attitude too. Because surly modeling will help them learn. Thank You for giving us second chances. In Your name I pray, Amen.

Further Reading: Luke 16:10-13

69

'Checed"
Sarah Lindsay

The Hebrew word "checed", is used in the Old Testament 247 times. It means lovingkindness, mercy, steadfastness, favor, and goodness. It is who God is.

There have been many times I have questioned the goodness and mercy of God. How is this loving when I am hurting so bad, or I see no end in sight to my situation?

That could be physical sickness, anxiety, work situations, care of a relative, homeschool, parenting, etc. Basically, anything beyond my control that doesn't go the way I prayed or the way I wanted it to go. It may seem like nothing good is happening, but the Lord is working. He is making me more and more like Him. He is molding me into His image.

Here are some things I challenge myself with during those hard times.

1. I need to remember who God is in the midst of my suffering. All the verses I have studied now about the lovingkindness of the character of God, His covenant love for me, His faithfulness to me; these verses help me in those times of silence or suffering. God never changes!
2. My prayers are being heard (Jere 33:3). I can give up, or I can be faithful in praying. The Lord's timetable is not mine, nor His plans mine.(Is 55:8-9)
3. I can pray for those around me going through hard seasons. I can send notes, I can come alongside and cry with them (Rom 12:15).
4. In II Cor 12:9 it talks about the fact that in our weakness, He is strong. I would say for myself that hard seasons are my weakest moments. Why? Because there is absolutely nothing I can do to fix the problem. I have to rely on the strength of the Lord. He is the one who sees the big picture. Rom 8:18 says it's not that the sufferings are not hard or difficult; but that in comparison to the glory which will be revealed to us, they are minor.

So think about the hardest thing you're going through. Encourage yourself with the promise that it will be worth it when you get to Glory and see the other side!

Know therefore that the Lord thy God, the faithful God, which keepeth covenant and mercy with them that love him and keep his commandments to a thousand generations.
Deuteronomy 7:9 ESV

Know therefore that the Lord your God is God, the faithful God who keeps covenant and steadfast love with those who love him and keep his commandments, to a thousand generations. Deuteronomy 7:9 KJV

Dear Jesus, Please help me focus my mind and my eyes on your love, mercy, and kindness to me. You are good, and you hear my prayers. Please encourage my heart with this truth. Thank you for your faithfulness and working in my life. In Jesus' name, Amen.

Further Reading: Psalm 17:7, 18:50, 25:6, 36:10, 59:10, 69:16, and Ps 94:18

70

You are Halfway
Trudie Schar

You made it to the midway mark of the school year!! Wahoo!!

The halfway point is always a great time to take an inventory of how things are going. I'm sure you are like me and some things are going great. . . While other things are NOT.

I like to change things up a bit for the second half of the year. I take a look at what went good and what went badly. I tweak the schedule, change the routine. I swap out when I help each girl or change up where we do school. Sometimes I have even changed curriculum at this mid point.

That is one of the huge benefits to homeschooling; we are free to change midway. (Yay!)

I also like to stop and take a moment to check my heart. How is my heart doing? Have I been doing this homeschool mama thing with drudgery or out of duty? Or have I been enjoying myself?

If it's out of drudgery and duty; Ugh. I'm sorry. I know the feeling. Go back to why you are doing it. Revisit the first half of the year and find the moments of joy. Perhaps do some of the same things that brought you joy the first time over again. Go back to Jesus and ask Him to fill you with purpose and renewed joy.

If you have been enjoying yourself, awesome! Check in with another homeschool mama and share some joy to her.

Celebrate the halfway mark with your children! They've been working hard too! Get excited! You are halfway there!!

Rejoice in the Lord always; again I will say, rejoice. Philippians 4:4 ESV

Thank You, Jesus! We've made it to the halfway mark! Show me if there are tweaks I should make for the second half of the year. Help me celebrate with my children, they've been working hard! Remind me why I'm homeschooling, and what has brought me joy. Restore that joy we had at the beginning of the school year. In Jesus' name, Amen.

Further Reading: Philippians 4:4-7

71

Are you Back from Christmas Break?
Trudie Schar

Christmas break as a homeschooler is FUN! You can start your break a little sooner. You can end it a little later. . . But then you go back.

Some years I've gone back with a flurry of energy. It's a new calendar year, there are new goals, things to look forward to too. I was excited and ready to get started!

Some years I've gone back tired. Tired of the school year. Tired of the curriculum and the routine. No energy to go back to doing things the same way on repeat.

The thing I've learned about January school is that: January is LONG.

January feels long because there are no big holidays or days off. And of course we just left a big holiday month. January also feels long because it is winter, and you tend to stay home and inside.

Sounds discouraging, right?

It is actually NOT discouraging! This LONG January is a good LONG!

January has become one of my very favorite months in homeschool because it is long. There are no distractions. There are no places to be. There are no big holidays to take off. January is the perfect time to stay inside and hunker down and get a TON of school done! I love the consistency of January. The routine. The less distractions.

If you are dreading this long month, I used to too... but now, I'm looking forward to it!

Happy January homeschooling, friends!

"But you, take courage! Do not let your hands be weak, for your work shall be rewarded." 2 Chronicles 15:7 ESV

Be ye strong therefore, and let not your hands be weak: for your work shall be rewarded. 2 Chronicles 15:7 KJV

Jesus, Thank You for this month of January. Help me to buckle down and use this time to really get back into a routine. Help me to be consistent. There are some heart issues we need to work on, give me wisdom to handle those correctly. Help us to enjoy being inside and at home this month. In Your name, Amen.

Further Reading: 2 Chronicles 15:1-7

happy **January**

72

When It Isn't July Anymore
Melody Plessinger

I don't know about you, but July is always my month that I feel reenergized and ready to go for a new year. It's the month (by the end) that I am ready to start planning what we are going to study. It's the month that many years I have finally had the courage to say, "Okay God... if this is what you are calling me to, I'm ready to do another year and I'm willing with your help."

July is my month to start looking with anticipation at the year ahead and think of all the fun we are going to have in the new school year. I start brainstorming and gathering and gleaning. I discard what didn't work and cling to what did and read up on new ideas or ask other veteran moms what worked for them or what they are enjoying. In my homeschool memoirs, July is full of fond memories.

But somewhere along the way, hard days have come and gone. High hopes get dashed. Curriculums get trashed. Toddler fits happen. Sickness plagues us. Marriages have tension. Teens push our buttons. Our expectations get lowered (even if perhaps they needed a little dash of reality in them). Plans get discarded or if not discarded yet they need some drastic changes... Let's face it life gets real, really fast about November... even if you last till January, there comes a day when you look around and think this wasn't the plan I had.

Where is the fun?

We haven't got enough done. The school year is only half way done and I have to somehow complete this year. I just want it to be July again... Oh, how I miss that anticipation and joy I had when looking ahead...

And yet in the middle of my plans the Lord's plan always comes through and His plan is always better!

Many are the plans in the mind of a man, but it is the purpose of the Lord that will stand. Proverbs 19:21 ESV.

There are many devices in a man's heart; nevertheless the counsel of the Lord, that shall stand. Proverbs 19:21 KJV

Lord Jesus, thank you so much for the opportunity to teach my children. Thank you, for the country we live in and the freedom we have because of that. Jesus, help me to be present in my year. When it's not the joyous times of anticipation help me to persevere and look to you for the strength to continue. Give me wisdom to plan a year that allows for grace. Help the children and I to be diligent in our studies and to have joy while learning. Help me to plan for fun in our year too, so that we can look back on our years with fond memories. Help me to not be too busy to miss out on the little moments. Lord, help me to reach my children's hearts as I teach them this year. In Jesus' name, Amen.

Further Reading: Hebrews 12

73

Speeding On The Way To Church
Trudie Schar

Every Sunday morning we are late to church.

Just the other day as I was taking my 4 year old to Sunday School she started crying. She looked at the Sunday School door and starting to cry she said "Mommy, Sunday School is OVER! I missed Sunday School!" (Cue tears)

I said, "No sweetie, that is what it looks like when we are ON TIME for Sunday school — The door is OPEN!" She had never seen the door open except for at the END. Every time she gets there the door is closed already. Every time she gets there we are LATE.

I HATE being late. It stresses me out, it makes me mad, mad, mad. It makes me yell and scream. I HATE being late.

SO week after week, Sunday was awful. I made enemies, and brought division between me and my hubby. Week after week. All the same.

Thankfully, I listened to God's voice.
Slowly, He got through to me.

First God really pinpointed me down and asked me WHY did I want to be early? Why was it so important to me? Why did it make or break my whole day? Those questions were hard to hear. I pondered them for several weeks. I found out I wanted to be on time:

#1 To look like I had my life under control to everyone watching me. (false, my life is NOT under control)

#2 To give a picture of a great Godly family.

#3 To be on the 'good list' (Is there a 'good' list at your church?)

I wanted to impress people. ALL my reasons included other people. Not my family. Not God. But just other people. People I didn't know. People I didn't spend time with. People I didn't have any relationship with.

The Holy Spirit went on to tell me that my relationships were more important than being early for church. My relationship with my family is more important than impressing people at church. My relationship with my husband is more important than putting on a good front. My relationship with GOD is more important than anything anyone else thinks of me. I had to make a decision.

Was I going to speed to church and stress relationships with people I loved
 while trying to impress people I hardly knew? OR... Was I going to slow down, make sure I enjoyed relationships with the people I loved and possibly be late to church?

Thankfully, God showed me which choice He wanted for me and my life.
No Impressing others. No being the first to church. No records broken.
No yelling. No tears. No unnecessary hurt feelings. No speeding on the way to church.

Is there anything you've been doing to impress people... but ruining your relationships with your kids in the process? Today is a good day to question your motives.

For am I now seeking the approval of man, or of God? Or am I trying to please man? If I were still trying to please man, I would not be a servant of Christ. Galatians 1:10 ESV

Jesus, there are some things throughout the week that stress me out. I often yell, whine, or get discouraged by them. Why? What about them makes me so uptight? Show me my motives behind it. If it is people pleasing... please open my eyes. Help me to hold my relationships with my husband and kids higher than my desire to please people I hardly know. Show me how to keep these relationships most important in my life. Thank you for giving me these relationships. In Jesus' name, Amen.

Further Reading: Galatians 1:9-10

74

1,000 Questions
Brittney Morris

There will come a day in your homeschooling journey, probably your first day honestly, when your child will ask you a question you don't know the answer to. You will feel a flash of "inadequate" run through you.

There will come a day in your homeschooling journey, at least within the first week I'm sure, when your child will know something that you don't know. You will feel a streak of "unequipped" ripple over you.

There will come a day in your homeschooling journey, most likely every day, when your kid is going to ask you 1,000 questions before 8 AM. You will feel a quiver of "unqualified" tear inside of you.

Days like these, and in my experience, most days fall into one of these three categories, we need to press into Jesus. We are not capable of doing this "homeschool thing" in our own power, or on our own understanding. We need God. If this is going to be sustainable, we need the presence of God to go before us, behind us, and with us.

On the days you have questions and doubts (and these days will be plentiful), remember that we have a Father that asks us to bring all our burdens to Him. He doesn't huff or get impatient when we have another question. He doesn't tell us to wait and get irritated when we bring Him our doubts. We serve a big, big God whose patience is unending, whose grace is sufficient. He covers our inequities with His blood.

His power is made perfect in our weakness.

But he said to me, "My grace is sufficient for you, for my power is made perfect in weakness." Therefore, I will boast all the more gladly of my weaknesses, so that the power of Christ may rest on me. 2 Corinthians 12:9 ESV

And He said unto me, My grace is sufficient for thee: for my strength is made perfect in weakness. Most gladly therefore will I rather glory in my infirmities, that the power of Christ may rest upon me. 2 Corinthians 12:9 KJV

My **grace** is sufficient for thee:

for my **strength** is made perfect in weakness.

Most gladly therefore will I rather **glory** in my infirmities,

that the **power** of Christ may rest upon me.

Heavenly Father, your goodness and faithfulness are unending. When I have come to the end of myself, there You are. You go before and behind and with me, all the days of my life. Help me to keep my eyes fixed on Your presence all around me. When I have questions, help me to lean in to ask them of you. When I have doubts, help me lean on you in dependence. Carry me, Lord, like a good shepherd carries his sheep when they are weak. In Jesus' name, Amen.

Further Reading: Proverbs 3:1-6

75

Try One More Time
Trudie Schar

Simon had worked hard ALL night and had not caught a single fish. Now Jesus asked Him to do something he knew— in his fisherman's brain — was clearly impossible. . . Throw in the net one more time. Simon said, "Master we have worked all night and haven't caught anything"

Have you ever said something similar to God? "God, I've been going to counseling sessions for years. I've been trying to homeschool for weeks. I've been trying to clean my house all day. I've been up with my kids all night. . . "

I've worked so HARD! And you ask me to try one more time. Can't I just give up?
I don't know, maybe it's just me... but I feel like I want to give up often. That time I was trying for a year to work through forgiving that person that hurt me ... but forgiveness just wouldn't come. When our remodeling projects on our "ugly house" wouldn't get done. When our homeschool fell apart. . . I'm tempted to just quit trying.

He said to them, "Cast the net on the right side of the boat, and you will find some." So they cast it, and now they were not able to haul it in, because of the quantity of fish. John 21:6 ESV

And he said unto them, Cast the net on the right side of the ship, and ye shall find. They cast therefore, and now they were not able to draw it for the multitude of fishes. John 21:6 KJV

Simon had worked hard all night and he had caught nothing. Yet, Jesus said to try one more time and Simon said, "Because you say so, I will let down the net." He threw in the net one more time. He caught fish, yes, but that's not all;

He finally SAW Jesus for who He was! The Son of God!

Simon's eyes were open! Praise God He threw in the net one.more.time.

Friend, Jesus wants me to throw the net in one more time. He wants YOU to throw the net in one more time. One more year of counseling, try that one last homeschool method you said you'd never do, give grace to that person that annoys you. . .

Maybe it's not about the result of catching fish at all. . . Maybe it's the miracle of seeing Jesus for who He really is. A miracle worker.

Let's whisper, "Jesus, because You say so, I will let down the net. I will try one more time."

Lord Jesus, I've been trying for weeks, yet it doesn't seem like I'm getting anywhere. You ask me to keep trying and it's hard to believe that anything will be different this time. Help me to try again. Remind me that it is not about results but about seeing YOU! Open my eyes to see You. Thank You, God for these experiences written in the Bible, so that we can learn from them. In Jesus' name, Amen.

Further Reading: John 21:1-13

76

Use Your Words
Trudie Schar

I have a little gal who whines. You know how that is right? She mopes and whines and sighs and moans. She doesn't say a word. Just mumbles and sighs and moans. She just makes noises.

Sometimes I already know what she wants. Sometimes I already know what is bugging her. I want her to tell me about it. I want to hear from her. I want a relationship with her.

I find myself telling her:

"STOP!! Just TELL Me with WORDS; what is the matter?"

"Just tell me with WORDS; what do you need?"

"Just tell me what you want! Don't whine!"

I find myself doing this in my own life.

I whine.

I moan.

I grumble.

I mutter.

I make noises.

I sigh.

God says to me:

Ask, and it will be given to you; seek, and you will find; knock, and it will be opened to you. For everyone who asks receives, and the one who seeks finds, and to the one who knocks it will be opened. Or which one of you, if his son asks him for bread, will give him a stone? Or if he asks for a fish, will give him a serpent? If you then, who are evil, know how to give good gifts to your children, how much more will your Father who is in heaven give good things to those who ask him! Matthew 7:7-11 ESV

"ASK and it will be given to you; seek and you will find; knock and the door will be opened to you. For everyone who asks receives; the one who seeks finds; and to the one who knocks, the door will be opened."Which of you, if your son asks for bread, will give him a stone? Or if he asks for a fish, will give him a snake? If you, then, though you are evil, know how to give good gifts to your children, how much more will your Father in heaven give good gifts to those who ASK him! Matthew 7:7-11 KJV

He doesn't want me to whine around. He wants me to ask.

He wants me to use words.

He wants to HEAR from me.

When my little gal stops whining around and actually TALKS to me and asks me.

Then.I.can.finally.help.her.

When I stop whining around and actually TALK to God

Then.HE.can.finally.help.me.

When I stop whining around and simply take my cares to my God, amazing things happen.

Yes, He already knows what I am feeling. He already knows what I'm whining about. However, He WANTS to hear from me.

He wants me to say it in words. He wants me to voice my feelings.

He wants a relationship with me.

When I go to Him with words. He can finally help me.

Often just in the sharing with Him I find relief.

Jesus, I've been whining around. Grumbling but not really asking. Though, I know you already know what's on my heart...today I'm going to use my words. Please.... In Jesus' name, Amen.

Further Reading: Matthew 7:7-11

77

To-Do's and Schedules, Oh My!
Charlotte-Anne B. Allen

Reading, phonics, math, science, history, Bible... and of course art, music, spelling, and handwriting practice. Check! All was in order for this week's work for my daughter and her two cousins... Oh, and don't forget the field trip Friday and make sure they write up their story about it afterwards. It's a good thing that their grandmother / aunt would be working with them for the beginning each week while I worked! She did much of the preparation and teaching.

Those years of rushing about and raising our now grown daughter are still clear in my memory. It was so easy to get overwhelmed when we became over-focused on our "to do's" rather than on the joy and excitement of learning. I mean, really! Wasn't I supposed to learn all of this so that I could then teach the material to them? What if I "missed" something? Surely that would scar them for life, or they'd fail their end-of-year evaluations!

Everyone would think that I was an awful mother. So, get out your schedule books students. It's time to hit the books and start checking things off our schedule... But thinking like this has a way of sucking all the joy out of our homeschooling experience, as well as adding unwanted stress.

What is a homeschooling parent to do? Isn't it important to be organized and set our goals?

I found in my long years of homeschooling, that joy comes not from rigid schedules and checking off schoolwork "to-do's" but from healthy routines with lots of flexibility. Each child is unique. As you consider each day, be prepared to shift what you have planned and make the child a part of the learning team, especially as they get older. Goals that they have helped to make are much more enjoyable. Take a lot of thought and time to consider your child's learning language.

What motivates them? What challenges them? Look at ways you can best support them and help them improve and grow. When you approach each learning experience with that in mind, learning becomes a shared experience and less of cramming as much as possible into an already full schedule.

We can take pleasure in the work God has given us

We can take pleasure in the work that God has given us, in the precious privilege of instilling in our child the joy of discovery, of accomplishment, and creativity. As the writer of Ecclesiastes said,

Everyone should eat and drink and take pleasure in all his toil—this is God's gift to man.
Ecclesiastes 3:13 ESV

As we contemplate those assignment books or lesson plans and "to-do's" may we look beyond the checks or circles and see the great opportunity to share with our child God's Word and the joy of learning.

God, I turn over to You my anxiety and stress about getting those schedules checked off. I feel so inadequate sometimes. Help me to enjoy these homeschooling years together. Thank you for this gift. In Jesus' name, Amen.

Further Reading: Ecclesiastes 3:9-13

78

Wanting Time Alone
Trudie Schar

Have you gotten long enough into your homeschool year that you have begun to yearn for time alone?

Maybe you are an extrovert and don't want it. But as an introvert this is about my biggest dream throughout the homeschool year.

It's not wrong to desire time alone. Jesus also spent time alone after a long day of serving.

And when he had sent the multitudes away, he went up into a mountain apart to pray: and when the evening was come, he was there alone. Matthew 14:23 KJV

And after he had dismissed the crowds, he went up on the mountain by himself to pray. When evening came, he was there alone. Matthew 14:23 ESV

Here's the deal... no one can help us get this time we long for unless we tell someone.

No one can help us get the time we long for unless we tell someone.

I've tried the "osmosis" method. Thinking maybe somehow sleeping in the same bed with someone would suddenly transfer the information. Then being disappointed when it didn't work. LOL

Here is what I learned:
I need to use words.

I'll give you a script "Honey, I need some time alone in the next week"
"I feel like I am suffocating, I could use an hour alone."
"I could probably be a better mom, if I had a little time alone."

But here's the deal. Your responsibility does not stop there. Once given the time alone you have to spend it wisely.

This means... DO NOT PAY BILLS. Do not work on answering emails. Do not fold laundry.
Be alone. Do something you enjoy. Something that FILLS you up.

Because if you waste this precious time, and do something that drains you... you come back worse than before. And your husband will remember that forever. (Or at least every time you ask him for free time for the next 5 years) Believe me. I know.

Jesus, you know what it feels like to serve all day and need to be alone. I am finding that I need that too. Please help me to express that need to my husband and children. Help me somehow find some time to make alone time happen. Show me what will refresh and revive me. Show me what activity will FILL me up so that I can come back ready to serve my people again. In Your name I pray, Amen.

Further Reading: Matthew 14:22-23

79

What IS your Identity?
Cheryl Kischuk

I am baffled as to why God STILL loves me. I continue messing up. I let anger reign. I remain stubborn in certain areas of my life. Why does God STILL love me? Yet, I see and feel Him saying "I love you" through many unexpected moments and experiences. I'm so undeserving.

Satan reminds me daily that I'm unworthy. It would be extremely simple to type out a page-long list of the types of things Satan yells at me on a daily or weekly basis. Examples include "You are incapable." "You'll never succeed." "No one appreciates you." "You're a fraud."

When I shared some of this with a friend recently, she asked a very poignant question. One that changed the trajectory of my thinking. Do you want to know what question she asked after I shared my list of lies Satan yelled at me? Dear reader, She asked, "What did you yell back?"

What did I yell back? I mean, I know Satan's hurtful statements were untrue. Yet, I don't think I realized how much I let them pierce my heart or identity. Knowing we have an enemy that intends harm is not something to just tolerate. This enemy studies our weaknesses and intends to come after our children, our marriages, and to hinder us in all we were created to be. I've decided not to simply be on the defense. I must be on the offense. I will not allow him to destroy my family.

Here is a portion of what I yell back now. I want you to hear me speaking right to you today.

You are God's masterpiece.

You belong.

You have direct access to God through the Holy Spirit

You are God's investment in His creation

You are forgiven.

You are saved by grace through faith.

You are free from condemnation.

You have been given a sound mind.

You have been given authority over the enemy.

You are hidden in a sheltered place under His wings.

You have a hope that is sure and steadfast.

You are pure in the eyes of God.

You know no weapon formed against you will prosper.

You are significant in Christ.

You have been chosen and appointed to bear fruit.

You are rejoiced over.

You are holy and dearly loved.

You will never, ever be separated from the love of God.

You can do ALL things through Christ who strengthens you.

You are a daughter of the Most High.

Dear sister, you have so much value to offer. You are beyond equipped and capable for the tasks set before you. Take those hurtful situations on with courage and clad-iron faith. You have the Creator of the universe on your team and He made you for this day!

"The thief comes only to steal and kill and destroy. I came that they may have life and have it abundantly." -John 10:10 ESV

"The thief cometh not, but for to steal, and to kill, and to destroy: I am come that they might have life, and that they might have it more abundantly." -John 10:10 KJV

Dear God, Thank you for who you created us to be. Thank you for giving us the Bible to remind us who we are when the enemy leads us astray. Thank you for being constant in our lives. Forgive us when we question our value and our purpose. We commit to bring you all the honor and glory with our lives. Fuel us with your supernatural energy and vision for what's to come. In your precious name we pray. Amen.

You can read more about Your Identity in Christ in Ephesians Chapters 1 & 2.

80

What Are You Supposed To Be Doing?
Trudie Schar

I am always saying, "What are you supposed to be doing?" I say it to my little gal who is tattling on her sister, instead of doing her dishwasher job. My big gal who is playing instead of doing her schoolwork. The nosey girl who is wondering why her sister gets to do something she isn't doing right now. The two that are fighting instead of cleaning up the family room.

I say, "What are you supposed to be doing?" to the two girls opening the huge bag of M&M's we just got from Sam's Club.

I say, "What are you supposed to be doing?" Over and over and over again.

So often, when fights arise, tattling starts, and grumbling is voiced, the child involved is NOT doing what they are supposed to be doing. EVERY.single.time.
I think. WHY?!!

WHY.have.you.stopped.doing.what.you.are.supposed.to.be.doing? Stopping and getting distracted with something else always leads to bad things so WHY did you stop doing what you are supposed to be doing??

Then I hear the Holy Spirit whisper the same words to me.

Ouch!

I'm guilty. Sometimes I stop doing what I'm supposed to be doing. I have fights, tattling, judging, gossiping and grumbling going on in my head. Or worse yet, coming out of my mouth.

This is a BIG one in my life.

I get so wrapped up in the issues around me. I start looking at the problems around me, church problems, other people's marriage problems, church leadership problems, America's problems, the problems in the world. I get stuck on this. I get discouraged. It doesn't seem to be handled how the Bible says it is to be handled. My family time, my homeschooling job, the housework it all suffers. I have STOPPED doing what I am supposed to be doing and I am focused on the wrong things. God comes to me and again gently whispers, "What are you supposed to be doing?"

When anything stops me from focusing on what I am supposed to be doing, Satan has me. I stop working for God. If I'm not working for God, then I'm working for Satan

I need to get back to doing what I am supposed to be doing.

What about you? What are you being called to do? "What are you supposed to be doing?" Stay focused on that.

Therefore, since we are surrounded by so great a cloud of witnesses, let us also lay aside every weight, and sin which clings so closely, and let us run with endurance the race that is set before us. Hebrews 12:1 ESV

Wherefore seeing we also are compassed about with so great a cloud of witnesses, let us lay aside every weight, and the sin which doth so easily beset us, and let us run with patience the race that is set before us. Hebrews 12:1 KJV

Jesus, sometimes I get distracted. I quit doing what I'm supposed to be doing. Bring me back into focus. I praise You for the Holy Spirit's work in my life. In Jesus' name. Amen.

Further Reading: Hebrews 12:1-2

81

Your Children's Heart
Trudie Schar

How are your children's hearts?

Often the way they are acting can tell you something about what their heart looks like. What has been a struggle lately? Have you seen any issues?

Homeschooling brings an unique opportunity for us to see our kids' hearts all day. Every day. With this chance to see them we are given the chance to mold them. We can point them in the right direction. We can call them out on what we see.

Perhaps it is neglecting their schoolwork.

Not finishing the papers completely.

Not trying very hard.

Ignoring instructions.

Not listening.

Skipping chores.

Sometimes this is an easy fix, they go for checklists. Give them a checklist and they will work for you. Sometimes it's that our kids are bored, they need a change up in the routine. Perhaps they need a goal to work towards. Sometimes something else is bugging them. Something deeper.

We have such an awesome opportunity to have plenty of time with them to ask about it. To dig deeper into what their heart is feeling and thinking.

Because we homeschool we get this chance. Are you taking advantage of the opportunity? Pay attention to your kids today. How are they really acting? How are they really doing? Is there a character trait they need reminded of?

So that thou incline thine ear unto wisdom, and apply thine heart to understanding; Yea, if thou criest after knowledge, and liftest up thy voice for understanding; If thou seekest her as silver, and searchest for her as for hid treasures; Then shalt thou understand the fear of the Lord, and find the knowledge of God.Proverbs 2:2 KJV

Making your ear attentive to wisdom and inclining your heart to understanding; yes, if you call out for insight and raise your voice for understanding, If you seek it like silver and search for it as for hidden treasures, Then you will understand the fear of the Lord and find the knowledge of God. Proverbs 2:2-5 ESV

Jesus, please help me to be attentive to the hearts of my children today. Help me see the things they are struggling with inside their hearts. I know sometimes it comes out in rebellion, anger, or other ways... but give me wisdom to know how to get to the root of the issue. The hurt underneath it all. Thank you for loving my children even more than I do. In Your Name I pray, Amen.

Further Reading: Proverbs 2:1-9

Good Enough
Nancy Beach

But he said to me, "My grace is sufficient for you, for my power is made perfect in weakness." Therefore I will boast all the more gladly of my weaknesses, so that the power of Christ may rest upon me." 2 Corinthians 12:9 ESV

I sat on the beach with another homeschool mama as our kids splashed in the water and threw the football. I was sharing with her my dilemma in trying to choose between two different History curriculums.

"I think I'll just do both," I told her.
"You're going to do what? Why?"

The answer I gave her was because I wanted my kids to have the best education. There were pros to both curricula and I wanted my children to be excellent.

That next school year I not only taught my children two history curriculums, I also added extra supplemental materials to their English class and their math class. I signed them up for soccer, and football, and youth group activities, and homeschool group activities. (Can we say, "overachiever?")

I ran myself and my children ragged from sun-up to sun-down. We weren't in elementary school anymore and I wanted my children to have the best chance at life.
When I look back on those days, I realize I was afraid to fail. So, I worked, worked, worked. If I could go back, I would hug my younger self and tell her to not sweat it. Then I'd tell her what I'm going to tell you now.

God knew what he was doing when he gave your children to you. You are able to homeschool them even if some days you don't feel like you are measuring up or doing enough. He doesn't make mistakes.

He knows you aren't perfect. And your homeschool day or week or year doesn't have to be perfect either. Your kids will be okay. Ephesians 2:10.

What has God called you to do today?

What has God called you to do today? Are your choices today from a place of fear or a place of love? Do what you are called to do in love. It will be enough.

Thank you, God, for equipping me to do what you've asked me to do. I pray you will help me keep my eyes on you and not on my efforts. Thank you for loving my children more than I do. Thank you for using my weakness to shine your strength into my life and my children's lives. In Jesus' name, Amen.

Further Reading: Hebrews 13:20-21

83

Zoned Out
Trudie Schar

Have you zoned out lately?

At our house we call it a "Trevey Trance" because I have a brother who is a thinker. As a little child he would stare off in the distance deeply thinking about something. If left alone he could stay in his bit of a trance for minutes upon minutes.

I've done this as a homeschool mom... not for minutes but for hours, days and weeks. Sometimes living in a world completely inside my head. Not having any idea of what is going on around me.

You too?

I'm coming to realize that Satan likes us to disappear into our own world. He wants us to grow blind to what is going on around us.

Because we stop seeing what is happening in our home.

The worst time I caught myself in this position was after months, maybe even a year of being oblivious. The thing that woke me up was my youngest daughter hitting me, trying to get my attention. (Kids hitting you is another discussion for another day.) This time it was totally my fault. I needed a good slap. It got me out of my trance and brought me back to reality. And boy the reality was a mess!

I realized I had been trying to disappear from the mess and run. But the deeper I zoned out the worse the mess got. Dear homeschool mama... don't zone out. I know it seems easier. But please don't. It just makes things worse.

Watch ye, stand fast in the faith, quit you like men, be strong. 1 Corinthians 16:13 KJV

Be watchful, stand firm in the faith, act like men, be strong. 1 Corinthians 16:13 ESV

Jesus, sometimes I just want to zone out. I admit I want to forget the drama swirling around me. Help me to not zone out. Help me to watch, pay attention and stand firm. I know when I zone out it is easy to miss something important going on inside my heart or my kids' hearts. Please help me to stay focused on our life right here. Help me not to miss the opportunities to share Your love with my children. In Jesus' name, Amen.

Read 1 Corinthians 16:13 & 14

84

Can I Glorify God with My Body and Eat Chocolate Too?
Jodie Wolfe

Or do you not know that your body is a temple of the Holy Spirit within you, whom you have

from God? You are not your own, for you were bought with a price.

So glorify God in your body. 1 Corinthians 6:19-20 ESV

Ouch! How many times have I read those verses over the years and felt prompted to get serious about treating my body as God's temple especially when I'm trying to be a witness for my children?

- I'll do something about that, Lord, after I eat up all this chocolate.
- I'll get up early and exercise tomorrow.
- I know I need more sleep, but I've wanted to see this movie for months. I'll catch up on my rest tomorrow night.
- I'll hurt my friend's feelings if I don't eat some of the snacks she worked so hard to make.

I would love to tell you I've succeeded through the years of honoring God with my body. But... don't get me wrong, there were some seasons when I ate healthy, exercised regularly, got a proper amount of rest, and felt great. However, that hasn't been the norm for my 50+ years.

All that changed about a year ago when I was diagnosed as diabetic. Suddenly my life was upturned. Now regularly exercising and eating a strict diet with carbohydrate limits is the norm. Long gone are the days of eating chocolate and snacks whenever I feel like it, or eventually getting to exercise.

At first, part of me bemoaned the fact that I should've made a change in my life when God's Spirit gently nudged me whenever I read those verses. Why did I take so long to be obedient?

One thing I'm learning through all this is to let go of the should've's, could've's, would've's. It doesn't do any good to cling to my past mistakes. Nor does it help my family. Instead, I can ask for forgiveness and use this lifestyle change as a way to honor God with my body, as scripture instructs.

When I long to reach for a candy bar I can choose to pray. I can thank the Lord for His many blessings in my life as I'm walking. I can find a way to encourage someone else who is struggling.

There are still times when I'll have a small amount of chocolate or a bite of a favorite dessert, but I'm learning the importance of moderation. I pray each day it'll get easier to focus on the Lord and not the foods I'm cutting out of my diet. I want to be faithful by allowing my body to be a temple for God's Spirit. I don't want to miss the blessings He has in store for me or my family.

Remind me, Lord that enjoying eating chocolate is fleeting but resting in You is eternal. Help me to remember my body is a temple. Allow my children to see You in my life. Make me more like You. In Your name, Amen.

Read 1 Corinthians 6:12-20.

85

A Graduate
Trudie Schar

The other day someone stopped by our house. As he hopped back into the work van he was driving, I thought "Wow! He is so little." But the next thought overtook the first one rather quickly. "Wow! He grew up so fast!"

Isn't that the truth!?!

Sometimes I look at my now-taller-than-me girl and think Wow! You grew up so fast! Yet, she is still so little compared to the big world out there.

So little yet so big
all at the same time.

So little yet so big. All at the same time.

Do you ever take a moment to look back at pictures you took years ago? Maybe do that. Just go back and remember how little they once were. Go back and remember and then look at them now. They've gotten so big!

Because we see them day in and day out we don't notice the little change over time. But WOW it is happening. Not too long and they will be that graduate in my driveway. . . driving off to their job.

{I realize this piece makes me sound old and sappy. It's ok. Maybe I am.}

Like arrows in the hand of a warrior are the children of one's youth. Psalm 127:4 ESV

As arrows are in the hand of a mighty man; so are children of the youth. Psalm 127:4 KJV

Jesus, it is hard to believe that my kids are going to grow up. That they will be graduating. They are so little. Yet so big. Help me train them in the way they should go. Help me prepare them for that day. Keep the big picture in my mind and on my heart. Because sometimes these days feel long. Thank You for providing for me. In Jesus' name, Amen.

Further Reading: Psalm 127

86

Do You Need Help?
Trudie Schar

Sometimes I like to hear my girls say, "Do you need help?" Maybe I'm about done with supper and I need the table set. Maybe I'm trying to get everyone out of the house and need something carried to the van.

Whatever I'm doing, I just love it when someone says, "Do you need help?".

I think our kids like it too.

When they are studying their spelling words, trying a long division problem, or reading a book. . . I tend to think it's always an appropriate question. Of course, we can't solve every problem, or help too much, they need to learn it for themselves. But the occasional "Do you need something?" Is worth asking.

This question shows that we care about what is going on in their world. It reminds them we care. It shows them we see. It builds up the fact that we are on their team.

And who of us doesn't want those things!?!

Do you need help?

Try it today sometime. Ask "Do you need help?"

Two are better than one, because they have a good reward for their toil. Ecclesiastes 4:9 ESV

Two are better than one; because they have a good reward for their labour. Ecclesiastes 4:9 KJV

Jesus, I'm so thankful I can do life beside my children. I can be here to help them when they need it. Help me to know when they need reminded that I'm here to help them. Show me how I can come alongside and encourage them. Guide me to the right balance of helping and having them do it themselves. In Jesus' name, Amen.

Further Reading: Ecclesiastes 4:9-11

87

Too Busy to not Make Time
Tara Maxheimer

My days are full of so many things to do.

Teach the kids, clean the house, do the laundry, make dinner…sometimes I get in this rat race and go 100 miles an hour to only go in circles. And while I've been busy all day, at times I feel like I get nothing accomplished.

When I have a day like this, I ask myself, "Did I spend time with God today? Did I connect to my power source? Did I make time to have a quiet moment to talk to Jesus and Be Still so I could listen and hear His voice?"

Many times, the answer to that question is no.

I make excuses in my mind that I just don't have time today or I allow myself to get distracted first thing in the morning by some task staring me in the face.

Martin Luther said, "I have so much to do that I shall spend the first three hours in prayer."

Spending time with Jesus first thing in the morning, sets the tone for the entire day. While the day's agenda may not change, the peace in my heart does. Jesus wants to give me His peace, but I must spend time in His presence first.

I have found He blesses me with getting so much more accomplished in a shorter period of time when I give Him the best part of my day. My heart is happier, my children are happier, I can be a better wife, and I can live this day with true joy in my heart.

O LORD, in the morning you hear my voice; in the morning I prepare a sacrifice for you and watch. Psalm 5:3 ESV

My voice shalt thou hear in the morning, O LORD; in the morning will I direct my prayer unto thee, and will look up. Psalm 5:3 KJV

Dear Lord Jesus, thank you for being a good and faithful God whose mercies are new every morning. Help me to spend quiet time with you every day so I can grow closer in my relationship with you, I can hear your Holy Spirit speak to me, and I can experience the peace you want me to have in my life. I want to walk this day holding your hand and never letting go. I pray this in the name of Jesus, Amen.

Further Reading: Psalm 46:10; Psalm 62:5-6

88

Faith Without Seeing
Trudie Schar

I keep opening up to the story of Thomas in the Bible.

You've likely read it but let me recap it for you. After Jesus rose the disciples were together and Jesus showed up! They believed. But Thomas was not with them. Thomas told the others that he was not going to believe until he had seen and felt Jesus for himself.

Jesus showed up about a week later, this time Thomas was there with them. He saw, he felt the nail holes in his hand, and he believed!!

This makes me think of you. If this is your first year homeschooling... I wonder if you have doubts? I wonder if you are being a little like Thomas and saying... "I will believe I can homeschool when I SEE it!"

I understand.

Yet, if Jesus was here I believe He would remind you that, "Blessed are those who believe without seeing."

Can you believe that you will be ok and make it through this homeschool year?? If you are believing in your own abilities — NO WAY! (I don't put one bit of confidence in my own abilities to make it through the year, in fact each year I get under my belt the more I realize I can't trust myself!)

BUT I can trust Jesus!

I can trust that if God called me to homeschool for this year... He is able to help me through it. I CAN indeed believe in what I've never seen before, when I know who walks beside me.

For we walk by faith, not by sight. 2 Corinthians 5:7 ESV

For we walk by faith, not by sight: 2 Corinthians 5:7 KJV

Jesus, sometimes it's hard to believe I will make it through this year. I know that I can not trust in my own abilities. But I can trust in You. I know you are walking beside me. Increase my faith, even when I can't see a way. Show me your presence. In Jesus' name I pray, Amen.

Further Reading: John 20:24-29

Developing Deep Roots
Cindy Coppa

Be encouraged! The Lord is on your side, mom. Remember that you are a work in progress and so are your children. Perfection? God's got that. (Psalm 138:8 KJV) You will make mistakes as a teacher of children and a student of the Lord. That's okay. You are human and you are His. God will fulfill His purposes for you and your children as you place your trust in Him and move forward. Do not despise small beginnings or the repurposed dining room table. You will grow steadily and bear good fruit if you stay in the process. Developing deep roots takes time.

Developing **deep** roots takes time.

Take a close look at that tree growing outside your window. You cannot see it growing, but it is. The process of growth that God started years ago in that tree continues day by day, moment by moment, enabling the tree to reach maturity and bear fruit or seeds for the next generation. You will too. Remember that perseverance and patience are fruits of the Spirit and an important part of our development.

Yes, the wind will blow and the storms of life may wreak havoc on your schedule from time to time, but deeply rooted trees and teachers will stand fast.

Stay in the process. Continue learning at Jesus' feet so your children can learn at yours. He is the ultimate teacher. You are in very good company. Be encouraged!

The LORD will fulfill his purpose for me; your steadfast love, O LORD, endures forever. Do not forsake the work of your hands. Psalm 138:8 ESV

The Lord will perfect that which concerneth me; Thy mercy, O Lord, endureth forever; forsake not the works of Thine own hands. Psalm 138:8 KJV

Lord, help me to stand fast. Root me deeply in your Word and establish my daily thoughts, emotions, lessons, and schedule. I place my trust in you to fulfill your plans for me as a mom and a teacher. Please keep me in the process and grow me by the power of your Spirit so that I will bear fruit for the next generation. I ask in Jesus' name, amen.

Further Reading: Psalm 138

90

Finding the Subject and the Verb
Trudie Schar

The other day I was watching one of my gals do her language worksheet. She was finding the subject and verb. The sentence went something like this. . . "In art class, we made animal masks."

That "In art class" part got a little distracting. It really has nothing to do with finding the subject and verb. You go into the sentence thinking it is about art class. But it didn't say "Art class was great." Or "Art class started late." No, the point was WE made animal masks. We is the subject. Made is the verb.

Those "in art class words" were a distraction from the real purpose. They complimented it, but they were not the whole point.

I think Satan tries to get us with this in our homeschool … distracted. He wants to get us off the main point of homeschooling. He wants to get us focused on something that was only meant to compliment it. Or perhaps focused on something that is not even meant to be a part of our life. Maybe it's just that the little details become our focus … the question of "when" finding the perfect time, or "how" what method to take, or "what" decision to make next . . . And it distracts us from the real purpose.
Ugh, how about feelings? How many times has fear, worry, discouragement distracted us? We get so worried it stops us in our tracks. It pushes us to quit. It scares us into not starting. It distracts us from doing God's will.

Satan loves to use distraction to get us off course. When we get distracted our eyes leave Jesus. Our mind stops thinking of bringing God glory! We stop physically doing the next step.

And Satan has got us.

I have to admit, I've found myself distracted many times. . . Comparing my homeschool beside someone else's. Looking around wondering why I'm doing what I'm doing. Wondering what the next step is.

Questioning if this calling to homeschool was really from God, and if so why doesn't it seem like I'm making any progress.

I found myself distracted. Distracted trying to sort out answers to all my questions. I want a plan, I want to know the end result. When the questions are bigger than the answers I get distracted.

And Satan has me.

You know maybe I don't need answers. Maybe I just need to take the one step in front of me. Maybe I just need to find that subject and verb. Maybe I just need to let the rest of the sentence go. Leave the distractions and just do the next thing.
What is Satan trying to distract you with today? Is he trying to add words to that sentence you are working on?

Remember you need to JUST find the subject and verb. Ignore the extra words, my friend.

No soldier gets entangled in civilian pursuits, since his aim is to please the one who enlisted him. 2 Timothy 2:4 ESV

No man that warreth entangleth himself with the affairs of this life; that he may please him who hath chosen him to be a soldier. 2 Timothy 2:4 KJV

Jesus, help me to not get distracted by the wrong things. Like finding the subject and the verb in a sentence help me to pick out what is important for our homeschool day and what is not. Help me to leave the "extra stuff" in their place. In Jesus' name, Amen.

Further Reading: 2 Timothy 2:1-7

91

Empty — But He Sees Me
Trudie Schar

I've been pouring out and pouring out. Day after day. Does anyone even notice everything I'm doing? Does anyone even notice me?

I feel so empty. I need a revival. I need three days to sleep.

I keep giving and giving and giving. Even in the night I keep helping these kids. And I'm glad to. But I'm empty. I need something to fill me back up.

You too?

You know, Satan likes it when we are empty. We start filling in the emptiness with grudges, anger, sadness...

Let's not stay there. Let's stop. Let's run to Jesus. He can fill us up.

One thought that gets me headed in the right direction is remembering God sees me.
He sees everything I've been doing. He sees all the times I pour out to my kids and the times I pour out to my husband. He sees when I share love even though I want to be receiving love. He sees when I give.

He sees me.
Friend, He sees you too.

The Lord looks down from heaven; he sees all the children of man; from where he sits enthroned he looks out on all the inhabitants of the earth, he who fashions the hearts of them all and observes all their deeds. Psalm 33:13-15 ESV

The Lord looketh from heaven; he beholdeth all the sons of men. From the place of his habitation he looketh upon all the inhabitants of the earth. He fashioneth their hearts alike; he considereth all their works. Psalms 33:13-15 KJV

Lord Jesus, I feel so empty. Every day, all day, pouring out and teaching my kids. Often I wonder if anyone notices all I am doing. I know you see me. Thank you. Help me to run to You to get filled up. I know You are the one with the living water that quenches my thirst. Help me to get filled up on You so I can keep pouring out to my children and husband today. In Jesus' name, Amen.

Further Reading: Psalms 33:13-22

92

Good Works
Jodi Leman

In some ways, I've both planned on homeschooling and was thrown into it at the same time.

Our family of six, with one on the way, came home from the mission field around the time of the COVID-19 shut down in early April. Because we were planning on coming back to the States to have baby #5 we were already planning on homeschooling. Then, with about a week's notice, we were encouraged to leave the mission field about 6 months earlier than we planned. So, homeschooling became a reality sooner than we expected.

Our plans changed so suddenly that I had nowhere to go with my mental state and my emotions other than to our Lord. It is not just about the homeschooling and the things I find myself doing. It is about the way I handle them in my heart. This verse has been given to me time and time again,

We are God's workmanship.

For we are God's handiwork created in Christ Jesus to do good works, which God prepared in advance for us to do. Ephesians 2:10 ESV

For we are his workmanship, created in Christ Jesus unto good works, which God hath before ordained that we should walk in them. Ephesians 2:10 KJV

I love both versions of scripture here. The ESV states that God prepared these works in advance for us to do. And the KJV says, "that we should walk in them." The homeschooling we have found ourselves doing, I believe is included in these works that God has 'before ordained' for us to do. That does not make the sudden changes any easier, but we can take refuge in our Lord. His grace is sufficient. His love is unconditional…for YOU!

Father God, I pray that I will never forget that you have given me these children as a blessing from your hands. I pray that I will be reminded often that homeschooling can be a good work that you have put before me. Thank you Lord, for my children and for this opportunity to serve you by raising these children for your kingdom. I love you Lord for your grace and your love that you lavish on me even when I am undeserving. In Jesus' name I pray, Amen.

Further Reading: Ephesians 2-3

93

A Fly on the Wall
Trudie Schar

I want to challenge you to be a fly on the wall for a moment.

How are things really going in your homeschool?

You know, oftentimes we are running through the day. Full speed ahead. List in hand. Knocking out all that needs to be done.

But what about the hearts of our kids?
What about the environment of our home?

Is our house a place where kids will thrive?

If you were a fly on your own wall... how would it be? Would you find a house that points to Jesus? A place where the Fruit of the Spirit abounds?

Not to sound cheesy or trite, but is your house a place that a fly would find relaxing? I just wonder.

Who we are at home... is way more important than who we are on Instagram and facebook . . . church and co-op . . . the library and grocery store. How is our home?

And let us consider how to stir up one another to love and good works. Hebrews 10:24 ESV

And let us consider one another to provoke unto love and to good works: Hebrews 10:24 KJV

Jesus, I want our home to be a place of refuge (not to a fly of course) but to my family. I want it to be safe, comfortable, and loving. I want the Fruit of the Spirit to be evident and abound. I want our house to be one filled with love. Show me how I can make changes, even just one little thing to adjust so that it is a haven. Thank You for Your forgiveness when our house hasn't been this way. In Jesus' name, Amen.

Further Reading: Hebrews 10:24-25

94

Alone Alone
Sue Bione

I'm pretty good at being an introvert. I am also what some would call an empath so I need my alone time to recharge. However, what I have found during this social distancing is I also need human contact, face to face, to keep me moving forward and feeling as if I have a purpose.

My calling is to be a therapist, a trauma therapist. I can hold space for those suffering so well and be able to turn it over and not carry their pain with me. What I didn't realize is that being able to care for my clients is best done in person. God has given me a gift of compassion and caring to walk through my clients with them, but "social distancing", (I prefer to say physical distancing), has left me feeling cold and dark about the use of my gifts.

Then I realized how many times I have been reminded to lean into God. I am never alone with God. God's gift to me can be used however He deems it. During this time, I am lucky enough to utilize the technology that we have. To continue to "see" my clients, walk with them and give them encouragement, regardless of being physically present with them or not.

Everything in life is judged by a unique perspective. All I need to do is continue to remember I am not alone. God is with me and has given me the greatest gift, to help others and I will not let physical distancing dampen my light; you see, for me light is life and I have been given a purpose for my life. I have been given light from God to carry forward in the darkness and I will continue to do so as long as I am able.

Behold, the hour is coming, indeed it has come, when you will be scattered, each to his own home, and will leave alone. Yet I am not alone, for the Father is with me. John 16:32 ESV

Behold, the hour cometh, yea, is now come, that ye shall be scattered, every man to his own, and shall leave me alone: and yet I am not alone, because the Father is with me.

John 16:32 KJV

Father, thank you for allowing me to lean on you when it feels as if everyone has gone home. I need your strength and comfort through these trying times. Father, place on my heart the knowledge that you are always there for me and I am never alone. In Jesus' Name, Amen.

Further Reading: John 16

95

Hungry for the Good Stuff
Trudie Schar

The last few mornings I've been getting up earlier. And boy I've been getting hungry!

I wish I could say I've been hungry for the good stuff; eggs, fruit, an omelet. But of course not, my list is more like toast, cream stick, or a leftover cinnamon roll.

You know, I'm not always hungry for the good stuff. But it's sure better for me. As I eat the good stuff I begin to desire the good stuff.

I think I see this inside my homeschool. When my kids eat good stuff... or learn good stuff, they want more. It's like it wets their appetite and they begin to crave learning.

As I've been learning this about myself, and seeing it play out in my kids, I am beginning to pray, "Lord, help me teach them to be hungry for the good stuff." I want them to be hungry for God and His Word. I want them to be hungry to learn about their passions and interests. I want them to be hungry to hone the talents they have.

The more we fill up up on the good stuff the more we crave the good stuff

The more we fill up with good stuff the more we crave good stuff.

The opposite is true too... When I fill myself with donuts and sugar I crave donuts and sugar.

What are you craving? What are you filling yourself with? What are you encouraging your kids to be craving?

A homeschool mama hungering after the good stuff is a mama who teaches her kids to fill up on good stuff.

Blessed are those who hunger and thirst for righteousness, for they shall be satisfied.
Matthew 5:6 ESV

Blessed are they which do hunger and thirst after righteousness: for they shall be filled.
Matthew 5:6 KJV

Jesus, help me crave the good stuff. Not just food wise, but what I put in my mind. What I read, watch, and learn. Help me to crave good things. Then help me to teach the girls to crave the good things. Thank you, that when we hunger after good things You fill us. In Jesus' name, Amen.

Further Reading: Matthew 5:2-11

96

Life School Interruptions
Trudie Schar

Have you experienced any interruptions in your homeschool day yet?

Whew! It seems that without fail there is something to interrupt us. At least once a week. Sometimes more.

Often we think of interruptions as a negative thing. But something I've learned is that it is not always bad.

One day, someone with young kids needed a babysitter at the very last minute. Yes, it interrupted our homeschool routine, but wow! It was a great experience for our girls to follow a toddler around and hold a baby. Learning to care for a baby is an awesome thing to know how to do. In some ways, it's more important than a couple lessons in geometry or memorizing all the presidents. "Life school" is what I like to call it.

"Life School" interruptions are just as good as school. Of course, not all of the interruptions are worthy of fitting in the "life school" category. Likewise going "life school" all the time isn't the best either, but "life school" definitely needs a place in the midst of our homeschool day.

When faced with an interruption as a homeschool mom we need to take a look at the interruption and evaluate it. Is it something that is valuable for our kids to learn? Or is it something we should say no to and pass on?

If it's something valuable that your kids need to know as they grow up and you feel up to it. . . by all means, take advantage of it and say yes to the interruptions.

But maybe it doesn't suit you. Or maybe it's not really a great learning opportunity. Or perhaps you haven't done math or reading lately. Then you should pass on the interruption. {Believe me, people get the idea that since we are home all the time ... that we have all the time.}

We need to find that balance of saying yes and no. We need to find that sweet spot of letting "life school interruptions" add excitement and joy to our day without letting them get out of control.

I will instruct you and teach you in the way you should go; I will counsel you with my eye upon you. Psalms 32:8 ESV

I will instruct thee and teach thee in the way which thou shalt go: I will guide thee with mine eye. Psalm 32:8 KJV

Jesus, help me find the balance between "life school" and bookwork school. Sometimes there are interruptions that are great opportunities for teaching my children. Sometimes the interruptions are just that. . . Interruptions. Please help me decipher which is which. Give me the gumption to say "no" when an opportunity comes up that doesn't fit into our schooling for that day. Thank You for guiding me. In Your name I pray, Amen.

Further Reading: Psalms 32:7-11

97

Maybe Normal isn't so Normal
Darcy Schock

Up until 2019 it was estimated that only about 3-5% (2.5 million) school aged children were homeschooled.

That's a pretty low percentage. Pretty "un-normal". Even knowing a lot of homeschooling families, with that kind of percentage, we can still feel like we are swimming upstream. Doubts can creep into our minds like:

Will I ruin my kids by choosing this unconventional path?
Why am I fighting this, I should just send them to school like all the other normal people?
What will people think of me when they see me in public with my kids who should be at school?
If I send them to school, they will graduate with all the other normal people. This path, it feels uncharted, scary.
I am not equipped to teach my kids like the school system is.

With the global pandemic of the Covid-19 virus, homeschooling has become much more "normal" for the time being. Even with the massive increase in 2020, the numbers still are only estimated at about 8.5 million kids out of 57 million. Statistically we are still in the minority. Still "un-normal."

While normal often feels like the safer path, I can't help but look at people in the Bible and how they were called to live a very "un-normal" life.

Noah built an ark when it wasn't raining.
Daniel and his friends ate vegetables when everyone else was eating meat.
Jesus, the King of kings, was homeless when all the other kings basked in riches.

I think as homeschoolers, we need to resist the temptation to look to "normal" for safety and guidance. We need to go back to our relationship with God. In this relationship we will be guided in ways far higher than our own logic or the "tried and true" path of culture.

True, the uncharted path feels scary. It takes more work to tune in each day to the guiding of the Holy Spirit. However, it is a custom path. A path that fits our family beautifully if we let it. Noah and his family were saved because of their obedience. Daniel and his friends came out even stronger than the other men. Jesus, well He reigns supreme in highest of highs. He owns everything. He is the richest man ever. The path that is "normal" Biblically, is listening for God's daily direction.

Let's tune our ears to God's voice and obediently follow His call in our lives. Let's stop looking for cultures "normal" to guide us.

"And your ears shall hear a word behind you, saying, "This is the way, walk in it," when you turn to the right or when you turn to the left." Isaiah 30:21 ESV

"And thine ears shall hear a word behind thee, saying, This is the way, walk ye in it, when ye turn to the right hand, and when ye turn to the left." Isaiah 30:21 KJV

Lord, I pray that you would guide me on the path that you have for me. I pray that I would tune out all the things that culture tells me is normal and tune into Your Holy Spirit to guide me. Thank you for giving me a personal teacher. Give me strength to follow, even when it is hard. In Jesus' name, Amen.

Further Reading: John 14:25-27

98

Summer is Coming
Trudie Schar

I'm sure that God was not thinking of a homeschool mom when He said these words... but I think I can say it is still a promise for us.

"Summer is coming!!"

God promises it.

God Promises it!

And when the Lord smelled the pleasing aroma, the Lord said in his heart, "I will never again curse the ground because of man, for the intention of man's heart is evil from his youth. Neither will I ever again strike down every living creature as I have done. While the earth remains, seedtime and harvest, cold and heat, summer and winter, day and night, shall not cease." Genesis 8:21-22 ESV

And the Lord smelled a sweet savour; and the Lord said in his heart, I will not again curse the ground any more for man's sake; for the imagination of man's heart is evil from his youth; neither will I again smite any more everything living, as I have done. While the earth remaineth, seedtime and harvest, and cold and heat, and summer and winter, and day and night shall not cease. Genesis 8:21-22 KJV

I hope that reminder gives you a boost of encouragement today. Summer is coming!

Thank you, Jesus, for keeping your promises every time! Thank you for this promise that summer is coming. You know what today looks like outside, it's dreary. We are so ready to see the sunshine again. So ready to enjoy being outside. Thank you for this reminder that the sun will shine again and the warmth will be back. Thank you for the seasons. In Jesus' name, Amen.

Further Reading: Genesis 8:15-22

99

Lessons Caught
Jodie Wolfe

I fondly remember many years ago when I was teaching our oldest son music lessons utilizing a curriculum called Color the Classics - Godly Composers. He was only five or six at the time. The course included a cassette tape to listen to along with coloring pages.

We studied great composers like Antonio Vivaldi, Johann Sebastian Bach, George Frideric Handel, and Joseph Haydn. While the music filled the background, my son colored the pages associated with the music, and I read to him the information about the compositions as well as the composer.

My younger son would have only been two or three at the time. He was in the same room with us, usually playing with toys and generally not paying attention to us... Or so I thought.

Shortly after we studied Antonio Vivaldi and listened to his piece entitled 'The Four Seasons' my youngest son was in the back seat of my mother's car. She was playing the radio and some classical music came on the station. He piped up and said, "That's Antonio Vivaldi." She was flabbergasted.

I was shocked when she relayed the story to me. I hadn't included this son in our lessons and because he was so young, I assumed he wasn't paying attention to what I was teaching my oldest. I was so wrong.

My mom spent her elementary years in a one-room schoolhouse. She's shared how much she learned as a youngster by listening to the lessons that were taught to the older students.

Some lessons we teach directly while others our children learn by our actions, or how we deal with another child or our spouse. They are always observing and learning.

I'm reminded of the scripture that says:

You shall therefore lay up these words of mine in your heart and in your soul, and you shall bind them as a sign on your hand, and they shall be as frontlets between your eyes. You shall teach them to your children, talking of them when you are sitting in your house, and when you are walking by the way, and when you lie down, and when you rise. You shall write them on the doorposts of your house and on your gates. Deuteronomy 11:18-20 ESV

Therefore shall ye lay up these my words in your heart and in your soul, and bind them for a sign upon your hand, that they may be as frontlets between your eyes. And ye shall teach them your children, speaking of them when thou sittest in thine house, and when thou walkest by the way, when thou liest down, and when thou risest up. And thou shalt write them upon the doorposts of thine house, and upon thy gates. Deuteronomy 11:18-20 KJV

Lord, thank You that You can use the lessons I teach my children directly as well as the ones I don't. Use me in the life of my children. Help them to see You in all I do. Open their hearts to the lessons You want to teach them. In Your name, Amen.

Further Reading: Deuteronomy 11.

100

The Messy Middle
Trudie Schar

I LOVE hot cocoa. Especially made with Almond milk, 3 pumps of Mocha, 1 pump of vanilla, 3 pumps of toffee nut syrup. Topped with whipped cream, Carmel drizzle and a sprinkle of salt.

I love sipping the cream, Carmel, salty mixture off the top of my drink. I adore the last few sips of cocoa at the bottom of the cup. Rich, thick, and chocolatey.

But you know what I've realized? I don't love the middle. The middle is just bland. Nothing exciting about it. Tasty? Yes, a little. But I don't drink it for the middle. I drink hot cocoa for the top and the bottom. Beginning and the end.

Kinda sounds like homeschooling.

I love me, the beginning . . . fresh pencils, new books, neat worksheets. Excitement. Like the yummy whip at the top of the hot cocoa.

I love me, the ending. . . Sorting the piles, finishing the grade, putting the old stuff out of site. The excitement of the finish and the promise of rest in the summer. Like the rich last sip of my hot cocoa.

But the middle is bland.

You are about in the middle of the school year. How are you getting through the messy middle? I tend to think you are surrounded by grading that you got behind on. Your housework is getting a bit neglected. The lessons have become checkmarks to just check off. The love of learning has gone a little stale.

There is a cure for the messy middle. As I see it you have two options:
* You can add more whipping cream to the top.

* You can share what you have so you get to the end faster.

My favorite is the first option; add more whipping cream to the top. You do this by adding fun to the school day. Take a break, go on a field trip, go get ice cream, go to the library or a coffee shop. Get new school supplies, have a movie day, or do school in a different room of the house.

The second option; share what you have so you get to the end; I'll be honest, it mostly works with hot cocoa and four daughters who want a taste. But really, asking a friend to pray for you, checking in with another homeschool mom, or going to a mom's outing is one way of getting through that messy middle. Sharing it with other women around you. Helping each other. . . It makes the messy middle turn to the rich creamy end quicker.

And a cup of good hot cocoa . . .at a quiet coffee shop. . . is never the wrong thing to try during the homeschool mama's messy middle. Wink wink.

"But you, take courage! Do not let your hands be weak, for your work shall be rewarded." 2 Chronicles 15:7 ESV

Be ye strong therefore, and let not your hands be weak: for your work shall be rewarded. 2 Chronicles 15:7 KJV

Jesus, help me to get through this messy middle. Show me ways that I can add a little excitement back into our school day. Surround me with people I can share my struggles with. Women that we can help each other get through the messy middle together. Thank You for the promise that You stay beside me. In Jesus' name, Amen.

Further Reading: 2 Chronicles 15:1-7

101

March is the Hardest Month of the Homeschool Year
Trudie Schar

Remember how I said that January was LONG. But in a good way?

March is here. And I have to warn you; March is not kind to homeschool mamas. March is LONG. The bad kind of long.

The newness of January and all its promises of a great new year is gone. The newness of the semester change and new adjustments is gone. The weather is still hanging on to winter (maybe I only speak as an Ohioan here wink) Everything inside of you and your children long for spring. March is long.

After doing this March homeschool thing for 10 years I've learned a thing or two.

1. Expect March to be LONG.

    Somehow when I expect it to take a while it goes faster. I tend to brace myself. It helps. Try it. Say to yourself, "March is going to feel long."

2. Plan for the long-ness.

    Plan something fun for March. Maybe a homeschool spirit week among your household. Plan an outing (even if it's to a warm coffee shop). Plan a family movie and popcorn night. Buy a fun treat at the grocery store and pull it out mid-month.

3. Be kind to yourself.

    You've been doing this homeschool gig for nearly 7 months; be kind to yourself. That's a long time to have a part time/full time plus job. It's ok if your house doesn't look perfect this month, or your laundry isn't completely folded every week. Give yourself grace.

It's March. I promise it won't last forever.

And after you have suffered a little while, the God of all grace, who has called you to his eternal glory in Christ, will himself restore, confirm, strengthen, and establish you.

1 Peter 5:10 ESV

But the God of all grace, who hath called us unto his eternal glory by Christ Jesus, after that ye have suffered a while, make you perfect, stablish, strengthen, settle you. 1 Peter 5:10 KJV

Jesus, March is a long month. I know that April is coming, spring is coming, the end of the homeschool year is coming; help me remember this. As we go through March help me find ways to brighten the days. Show me a couple ways that I can add excitement to the month for my kids. Help me be merciful to myself, sometimes I am my own worst enemy. Thank you, Jesus, for promising to restore, confirm, strengthen, establish me in this calling. In Jesus' name, Amen.

Further Reading: 1 Peter 5:6-11

102

Stop, Mama, And Look Them In The Eyes
Tandy Sue Hogate

As a homeschool mom, the days can be incredibly busy. It's easy to get to the end of the day and realize that you haven't taken the time to just be with your kids, listening, looking them in the eye, reassuring them of just how loved they are.

Sweet mama, oh how I understand just how full and exhausting your days are. Everything you do, every day, is essential. I want to gently remind you to make sure that you take a moment every day with your children one-on-one. Look them in the eye. Talk with them. Listen to their heart. Pray over them.

Your child will be reassured of your love for them. Furthermore, this is also a fundamental building block for them to understand the love and care of their Savior. Here is an incredible thing about these deliberate moments that I found to be true. The time spent with my kids individually served as a balm for my own heart, spurring me on throughout the day.

You see, God has called you to homeschool your children for their benefit and yours. He loves your family and wants a relationship with each of you. He will use homeschooling as a powerful tool to draw you and your children closer to Him if you allow Him to direct your days.

Trust in the Lord

Trust in the Lord with all your heart, and do not lean on your own understanding. In all your ways acknowledge him, and he will make straight your paths. Proverbs 3:5-6 ESV

Trust in the Lord with all thine heart; and lean not unto thine own understanding. In all thy ways acknowledge him, and he shall direct thy paths. Proverbs 3:5-6 KJV

Jesus, our heart's desire is always to follow you, but that is not always an easy or clear path. Father, please direct our hearts and minds to Your perfect and loving plan. Thank you for loving our family more than we can comprehend. Please fill us with your supernatural love and wisdom. In Jesus' name, Amen.

Sweet mama, I would like to encourage you to read the entire chapter of Proverbs 3. It is packed with wisdom and insight.

103

Homeschooling is a Mission Field
Trudie Schar

There is no denying it. I was feeling jealous.

Once again, I was in a conversation that started something like this ... "Oh did you hear that Mark and Brenda are moving to plant a small church?"

These conversations usually leave me wishing God had clearly called me to some special work. It leaves me wishing people would be able to look at me and acknowledge that I have a hard assignment. I wish I left people with thoughts of, "She will be good at that!" or, "She will be perfect for that mission field!" Rather, I'm left with an empty feeling; a fear of being useless.

Then one day it happened.

I was listening to a homeschool convention replay on one of my walks. The speaker said, "Homeschooling is your mission field." I can remember where I was standing on the sidewalk. (My neighbors probably wondered about me, stopping right there dead in my tracks.)

Someone just said I was a missionary.
A dream comes true.
Someone had just called out the fact that homeschooling is a mission. All those things said about others, the reactions that I overhear with such jealousy, could be spoken again with my name attached.

As I thought about this, I have realized that homeschooling is indeed a mission field. Perhaps even the most important one on Earth.

Just like other mission fields this homeschool thing is full of unknowns and hard days. In the homeschool mission field we suffer hunger, thirst, lack of sleep, and changing seasons. Sometimes we won't feel safe;

our children might resemble monsters or we might be an emotional mess. Sometimes the conditions get quite messy: play-dough, dirt, glitter, and Cheerios surround you. Sometimes we may experience challenges with the mission board, overseer, or the missionary by your side...aka your hubby.

No matter what obstacles you face, there are still joys on this mission field. First, the great joy that only comes from being in the center of God's will. You touch people's lives. You bring the light of Jesus to your little people. You, dear homeschool mom, are a missionary.

And who better to serve? Who better to minister to than to your own family; your husband and your children. This special place God has called you to is your mission field.

And he said to them, "Go into all the world and proclaim the gospel to the whole creation."
Mark 16:15 ESV

And he said unto them, Go ye into all the world, and preach the gospel to every creature.
Mark 16:15 KJV

Jesus, I know that you find homeschooling important. I know You have called me to be right here. Sometimes the stuff I do feels little and un-important. Help me see that this is a mission field. That this molding and teaching my children is important work. Help me to remember this command to share Jesus. Encourage me when the hard stuff comes. In Jesus' name, Amen.

Further Reading: Mark 16:14-20

104

Grace is Sufficient
Cynthia Stoller

Dear Wise One (those who have graduates),

School was going so well! Chores were done before breakfast. Devotions were done before school. And everyone was finished with their work by 3PM. And then, life happened.

Daddy left for work out of state and is not going to be home until the weekend. The baby decided he needed a few more teeth, and the nights have been rough! His four year old sister thinks I can function with little sleep and gets up at 5 every morning. The younger boys know what is expected for chores, but have neglected them. We are lucky to get a little reading, writing, and math done with each child everyday. Help! What advice do you have?

—A struggling homeschool mom

But, he said to me, "My grace is sufficient for you, for my power is made perfect in weakness." Therefore I will boast all the more gladly of my weakness, so that the power of Christ may rest upon me. 2 Corinthians 12:9 ESV

And he said unto me, My grace is sufficient for thee: for my strength is made perfect in weakness. Most gladly therefore will I rather glory in my infirmities, that the power of Christ may rest upon me. 2 Corinthians 12:9 KJV

Life can be really hard!

Just when it seems you have it all together and everything is going well, things happen.

Children get sick. Daddy goes to work. Unexpected visitors show up. People die. Babies are born. Momma gets sick. Children have accidents. The list can go on and on. I don't know how you react to life's difficult times.

The more I try to get my act back together, by myself, the more frustrated I become. I can only rely on Jesus to give me grace to wake up and do the needful things of the day. The needful things for me are: something to eat, a load of laundry in the washer, and a little of the three R's with each of the kids. Slow down, figure out what the needful things are for you, and trust in Jesus' grace, power, and strength to get you through.

———————————

Slow down and trust

———————————

Dear Jesus, calm my troubled spirit, quiet my heart, and give me wisdom to go on! Life is hard right now! I need the grace, thy strength and thy power to be the mom I need to be. Give me peace in doing the needful things and leaving everything else in Thy hands. I want to glorify Thee in these difficult times! In Thy name, Amen

Further Reading: 2 Corinthians 12:7-10

105

The Tired Mom's Easter
Trudie Schar

Tired Mama, I see you, getting up this Easter morning, picturing a perfect day with your family. I know you wanted to get up early and finish cleaning up the family room and wash off the kitchen table. I know you were too weary to do it last night before bed. Unfortunately, due to children being up in the night, you felt more tired this morning than you did before bed last night.

Instead you slept in.

I know you wanted all your kids to be matching so you could take the annual picture. You had clothes, all but that one shirt laid out. You cleaned up the messy pigpen bedroom yesterday just so you could insure that the shirt would be in the laundry. For sure. How were you to know that the missing shirt would stay missing till way past church time. Maybe because you knew. When your daughter wore it all week pretending to be a princess, you knew that it would never be seen again. You knew, because moms are like that.

You knew you wouldn't have a chance of making it to the sunrise service. Not a chance. Still you feel like a failure at first glance of the clock.

Who knew your daughters would decide they were going to wear a different outfit on this Easter morning. Even though they've had outfits picked out for 4 months for this day. Who knew.

I see you, tired mama. Hang in there. Easter isn't about being perfect. Easter is about finding that the only Perfect has risen! Jesus! Jesus is our perfect. A perfect love story.

So mama, go have a good cry in the shower.

And then rejoice, because we have HOPE!! Our Lord is risen!

For God did not send his Son into the world to condemn the world, but in order that the world might be saved through him. John 3:17 ESV

For God sent not his Son into the world to condemn the world; but that the world through him might be saved. John 3:17 KJV

God, thank you for sending Your Son to die on the cross for our sins. Jesus, thank you for submitting to that death so that I might be saved. Help me focus on that instead of the way things down here go sometimes. That is all. In Jesus' Name, Amen.

Further Reading: John 3:15-18

106

Little Gifts From God
Trudie Schar

I found a nail on my garage step the other day.

It seems kind of silly but I have been needing a little nail for weeks. I had a clock sitting there by the wall just waiting to be hung. All I needed was a little nail.

Nails are like pens, they are gone when you need them and abundant when you don't.

When I saw the perfect nail on the garage steps I had almost forgotten I needed one. I had not prayed for a nail (how silly, right?) But it was just what I needed. It was an answer to a prayer I didn't pray.

A little gift from God. A little way that He shows that He still cares and He still sees. A little way He shows me He sees the little details, even if I have forgotten.

I wonder if sometimes we miss these little things because we are so busy wrapped up with our list to do. I wonder if we miss the little acts of love that God does towards us. Sometimes we may never know, the accident that was prevented, the injury we just about had, or the way someone had just prayed for us right when we needed prayer.

I **wonder** if we miss it.

I wonder if we miss it.

Look for Him throughout the day. Is he showing up in a little thing? Is there some little way that he's trying to remind you that he remembers you and he cares for you?

He's providing for you in the little details. I pray our eyes are open to see the little acts of love from God today.

Why, even the hairs of your head are all numbered. Fear not; you are of more value than many sparrows. Luke 12:7 ESV

But even the very hairs of your head are all numbered. Fear not therefore: ye are of more value than many sparrows. Luke 12:7 KJV

God, thank You for noticing the small things about my life. Help me to see them as little gifts from You, rather than rushing past in busyness. It seems overwhelming that You know the number of hairs on my head. Wow. To think You know so very much about me. Thank You. In Jesus' name, Amen.

Further Reading: Luke 12:4-7

107

Broken Jar
Toni Studer

When hot liquid is poured into a glass jar, it will probably break.

However, if you put a metal spoon in the jar and then add the hot liquid, it won't break. The metal takes some of the heat away from the water.

Homeschool moms are like a glass jar.

As a homeschool mom, you have a lot of "heat" that you deal with on a daily basis: school work needs done, papers need graded, dinner needs cooked, the kitchen needs cleaned, laundry needs folded, groceries need to be bought, bills need paid, husbands need encouragement, kids need boo-boos kissed, and the list goes on.

If mom doesn't have God's Word filling her soul each day, it's like pouring hot water into an empty glass. It will break! God wants to take some of the heat off of you so that you don't break.

God's Word is so important to our daily life. We need to allow God's Word to fill our heart and soul, so that when the daily pressures start to build up, we can withstand it with grace and dignity. We can be the mom our kids need and the wife our husband needs. Let's saturate our thoughts with God's promises.

Don't let the pressures and temptations of this world take over your thoughts.

Philippians 4:8 ESV says,
Finally, brethren, whatsoever things are true, whatsoever things are honest, whatsoever things are pure, whatsoever things are of good report; if there be any virtue, and if there be any praise, think on these things.

Finally, brethren, whatsoever things are true, whatsoever things are honest, whatsoever things are just, whatsoever things are lovely, whatsoever things are of good report; if there be any virtue, and if there be any praise, think on these things. Philippians 4:8 KJV

What a beautiful picture of a mind and heart filled with things that are pure, and lovely!

What an incredible relationship with God we can have when our minds are set on things above! What a sweet blessing we can be to our family when our focus is only on what is true and honest.

Let's aim to center our thoughts on these things and see that our cup can stay strong and withstand whatever is thrown at us! We can be like the Proverbs 31 woman, who is said to have, "strength and dignity as her clothing" (Prov. 31:25 ESV), who "opens her mouth with wisdom, and the teaching of kindness is on her tongue" (Prov. 31:26 ESV), and who's "children rise up and call her blessed; her husband also, and he praises her" (Prov. 31:28 ESV).

It really is an attainable goal!

Heavenly Father, I pray that you will give me strength to withstand the pressures of daily life and the hardships of this world that we live in. Fill me with your Spirit and give me the desire to dig into your Holy Word daily! Lord, you are so gracious and forgiving of my shortcomings. Thank you for always bringing me back to you. Help me to allow your Word to guide my life and fill my heart and mind. In Jesus' name, Amen.

Further Reading: Proverbs 31:10-31

108

Reset
Trudie Schar

Have you found yourself dreading homeschool? If so, why?

Is it the kids? Are they whining around? Have they picked up complaining? Are there some character issues that need addressed?

Is it the house? Is there clutter everywhere? The laundry undone? Does the kitchen need a good cleaning up?

Is it your spouse? Does he need some extra attention? A meal at a restaurant? A date night away?

Is it you? Do you just need a moment of quiet? A day off school to work on something other than worksheets and grading? A walk in the quiet sounds of nature?

Here is your permission. . . Take a day off!! Maybe even a week!

Reset.

The simple reset is POWERFUL! Try it. Take a moment to get stuff back to a manageable state. Take a moment to rest. A moment to reflect. A moment to let the school work and all those expectations of yourself go. Get into God's Word. Pray your heart out. Rest for a moment.

Hit the Reset button.

I promise that if you try this; without feeling guilty for doing so. . . you will return back to homeschool ready to go again.

"Have I not commanded you? Be strong and courageous. Do not be frightened, and do not be dismayed, for the Lord your God is with you wherever you go." Joshua 1:9 ESV

Have not I commanded thee? Be strong and of a good courage; be not afraid, neither be thou dismayed: for the Lord thy God is with thee whithersoever thou goest. Joshua 1:9 KJV

Jesus, sometimes things are overwhelming. I feel like I'm just going along swimming against the current. Help me take a moment to reset. Show me how long of a break we need, and what I should focus on during the little break. Help me (and the kids too) to be able to catch up on the things that have been let go; character issues, household chores, time with each other, and time with You. Help us to be able to reset and have another go of it. I praise You, that You are always ready to be with us wherever we go. In Jesus' name I pray, Amen.

Further Reading: Joshua 1:1-9

109

Do it With a Will
Jessica Heinlen

My husband's grandmother was a very influential person in my life during my early years of motherhood. She was a German war bride and came to America after World War 2. She knew how hard life could be and we would usually call each other every morning.

If I was having a rough morning with the kids she would tell me to "just love them" and would quite often quote the verse from James 4:8, draw nigh to God and he will draw nigh to you.

She was such an inspiration to me and the kids. She loved to have our kids come and visit with her one on one and bring something to work on with her. Whether she would help them with their writing or teach them how to make her favorite apple kuchen, she would always tell them to, "do it with a will".

No matter what it was, she always encouraged them to do their best and nothing less.

Draw nigh to God and He will draw nigh to you.

His grandmother has been gone now for a few years but her words of truth still resonate in my mind. On those days when I've changed the third poopy diaper in a row, taught phonics until I was blue in the face, and felt as though nothing I've done or said has really mattered at all, I'm reminded of what's truly important. To do everything with a will, love with all my heart and to continue to draw close to God.

Draw near to God, and he will draw near to you. James 4:8 ESV

Draw nigh to God, and he will draw nigh to you. James 4:8 KJV

And he said to him, "You shall love the Lord your God with all your heart and with all your soul and with all your mind. Matthew 22:37 ESV

Jesus said unto him, Thou shalt love the Lord thy God with all thy heart, and with all thy soul, and with all thy mind. Matthew 22:37 KJV

Lord, thank you for never leaving me or forsaking me. When this homeschooling life is hard and messy, all I have to do is draw close to you and you will draw close to me. Your love never fails. Help me Lord to love you with all my heart, mind, soul and strength and in turn, help me to love my child (ren) the way you do. Thank you for your perfect love. In Jesus' name. Amen.

Further Reading: Romans 8:35-39

110

Saying No
Trudie Schar

This morning I was a bit off — Triggered some would call it. Everything was going wrong. It was an Eeyore sort of day. It had started out a fine day, so I knew it was something that happened. When I took a step back and looked at it, I realized the issue.

I had to tell someone no, we couldn't help them. We already had prior commitments.

I'm a people pleaser and I'm afraid people won't like me if I turn them down. So telling someone no is definitely something that can set me off. Just putting my finger on that underlying reason of why I am stressed, is always the first step of getting back to normal.

In this case, I then went back through the reason and asked myself why did I say no? I have to go through the reasons again and tell myself the truth. The project she wanted help on; is it my responsibility? Is it in my fence, my boundaries?

By stressing and letting it bother me and make me feel guilty; I am beginning to carry her load. I'm picking up something imaginary and putting it in my fence to deal with.

By the way, the other person doesn't even know I'm still worried about it. It is only hurting me. And I was letting it ruin my day.

What about you? Do you have something gnawing at your mind today? What is it? Figuring it out is truly the first step towards moving on. Once you've figured it out go through what is true about the situation. Tell yourself the truth. Then move on.

Don't let it ruin one more moment of this precious day.

Finally, brothers, whatever is true, whatever is honorable, whatever is just, whatever is pure, whatever is lovely, whatever is commendable, if there is any excellence, if there is anything worthy of praise, think about these things. Philippians 4:8 ESV

Finally, brethren, whatsoever things are true, whatsoever things are honest, whatsoever things are just, whatsoever things are pure, whatsoever things are lovely, whatsoever things are of good report; if there be any virtue, and if there be any praise, think on these things. Philippians 4:8 KJV

Jesus, sometimes I have things that I just keep thinking about. Things I keep hashing out in my mind. Help me to stop and recognize what is really the problem, what triggered me. Then teach me to repeat the truth over in my mind. Help me to be able to move past those thoughts and feelings so I can be fully present for my kids today. Thank You for giving me this list of things to keep on my mind; true, honest, just, pure, lovely, good report. Help me think on these things. In Jesus' name, Amen.

Further Reading: Philippians 4:1-8

111

We are a Team
Trudie Schar

Something I've heard from homeschool moms is this idea of "me versus them". The feeling that homeschool is a fight between parents and the kids. If I'm honest, I've felt this fight, too.

At times it has felt like I'm the bad guy making them do all this work. And when it is that way our homeschool life is rough. It affects our family life, too. And it's miserable.

To combat this, I've made the "lessons plans" become the bad guy. When the lesson plans are the "bad guy" I can move to my rightful place as a team member. How do I make this switch? It's in how I present it. I say statements like:

"Ok, what does the plan say we are to do today?"
"Ugh, looks like they want you to do a chapter checkup today. . . We will get through it!"
"Hey, we are a team! I'll sit here and watch you do it!"
"I'm here to cheer you on."
"Oh fun, the paper says we get to read this story today."

As a kid having someone beside you to cheer you on is a whole lot better than a bossy teacher. . . Yes, you really are both. You are the one putting the "to-do" list on the lesson plans; but somehow if you blame the lesson plans you aren't the bad guy.

We are a Team

I don't know maybe one of these days they will realize I'm the bad guy and the teammate, but for now I'm not complaining.

Therefore encourage one another and build one another up, just as you are doing. 1 Thessalonians 5:11 ESV

Wherefore comfort yourselves together, and edify one another, even as also ye do. 1 Thessalonians 5:11 KJV

Lord Jesus, I want to be an encourager for my kids. At times it feels like I'm the bad guy, handing out all the work to them. Help me make a switch in the way I present it to them. Help me show them I am on their side, that I am cheering them on. I Thank You that You are this to me, You are right by my side cheering me on. Help me to be that person for my kids. In Jesus' name, Amen.

Further Reading: 1 Thessalonians 5:4-11

112

He IS our Refuge
Debbie Gibson

Do you find it hard to just be still?

Busyness is all around. There's so much to do. There are people to care for, laundry to fold (yes, you do need to fold it!), dishes to wash, toilets to scrub, and on and on. Everyone and everything cries out for your attention.

The world tells us we need to take time for "self-care," to put ourselves first sometimes. But that's not natural for a mother. We give and give, meeting the needs of everyone around us--until we're empty. Then we try to give some more—but there's nothing left to give.

The truth is, the most important thing for us to do to care for ourselves (and ultimately for those whom we love) is to rest our souls. We need to immerse ourselves in the Word of God—and in His presence--daily.

Don't let your Heart be troubled.

Don't let your heart be troubled, Mama.

We can—dare I say we must—take refuge in the shadow of His wings. Jesus tells us to come to Him when we labor and are heavily burdened, and He will give us rest for our souls. He tells us to learn from Him…and we will find rest for our souls. (Matthew 11:28-30)

Be merciful to me, O God, be merciful to me, for in you my soul takes refuge; in the shadow of Your wings I will take refuge, till the storms of destruction pass by. Psalm 57:1 ESV

Be merciful unto me, O God, be merciful unto me: for my soul trusteth in thee: yea, in the shadow of thy wings will I make my refuge, until these calamities be overpast. KJV

Heavenly Father, thank You that You are our Refuge. Whatever the status of the world around her, You promise rest for the soul of the heavily-burdened mama. Please help the harried mama reading this to take refuge in You, to rest in You, knowing that You are sovereign, and all things are determined by Your hand. Amen.

Read Psalm 40, and meditate on those words of our "Help and Deliverer."

113

Not Changing the View, but the Perspective
Trudie Schar

Our large picture window was a mess. Handprints, dog prints, smears, water marks... It was visibly dirty for about a week. Finally I got the energy to get it cleaned.

You know, the view I could see out the window didn't change at all; but my perspective changed! Rather than seeing that window and thinking "Boy! I have got to clean that" or "Ugh, I haven't got that done yet." Or "Trudie, you are such a loser, why can't you keep your windows clean?"

Rather than look at the window and think all that; I could enjoy the view.

Sometimes I think we have a "dirty window" in our homeschool life. Something that just needs a bit of tending to. I'd tend to say it wouldn't even take that long to deal with it. But we just put it off. And beat ourselves up for not getting it done.

I tend to think taking care of that "dirty window" in our homeschool world would change our perspective.

What is it for you right now? A pile of papers to grade? A messy bookshelf? A computer that needs backed up? New batteries in the clock? That picture on the wall straightened?

What's been annoying you lately? Go take five minutes and do it. It won't change your view, but I'm going to guarantee that your perspective will look a bit brighter.

For now we see in a mirror dimly, but then face to face. Now I know in part; then I shall know fully, even as I have been fully known. 1 Corinthians 13:12 ESV

For now we see through a glass, darkly; but then face to face: now I know in part; but then shall I know even as also I am known. 1 Corinthians 13:12 KJV

Thank you Jesus for the times we can see things more clearly. Help us to be able to take care of those little things that get in our way. Like the messy window, help us to take care of those things so we can see clearly. Give us strength to do those jobs we dread. In Jesus' name, Amen.

Further Reading: 1 Corinthians 13:11-13

114

Go to the Source That Never Runs Dry
Jodie Wolfe

How do you have a successful homeschool? With the increase of homeschoolers in the United States, a plethora of materials and resources are being made available. Books, magazines, online seminars and support groups can all be used in the quest for success.

But often all these sources don't have all the answers. Then what? One curriculum might work for one of your children, but not for all of them. It's easy to become discouraged and be guilt ridden.

You may start to question yourself and your abilities. You see magazine articles of families with smiling faces, organized homes and seeming to have it all together. You look at your home and see cereal on the floor, a glass of spilled milk on the table and on your homeschool planner. One child is in pajamas, another is crying and tugging on your shirt needing help to tie their shoe and you wonder if the toddler will ever be potty trained.

What do you do with the child who can get a perfect score on a spelling test but not retain it a day later? How do you teach your older children when you weren't a good student yourself? How can you do science experiments that are geared for a well equipped classroom? How do you know if you're covering everything? What if your child graduates and you forgot to teach them something major?

Perhaps you have children like me. One son excelled naturally with academics. He didn't have to study hard and required very little guidance from me. My other son was designed differently. He's just as bright. He tends to be more of a hands-on learner. He wasn't great at self motivation and required more work to keep him on task.

I know God wired each of my children uniquely, but through the years there were times when I beat myself up with guilt. I can't take acclaim for how well my child did his schoolwork when it was a natural ability God gave him. Just as I can't take credit for his achievements, nor should I take guilt for another child's struggles. Instead, I need to ask God's direction on how best to motivate and help him achieve.

Through all my years of homeschooling, I loved reading various homeschool materials. They can be a real source of encouragement. But to truly have a successful homeschool, our ultimate authority needs to be Jesus Christ. Only He has the answers to all the questions and concerns that we face with educating our children. Look to Him daily.

But seek first the kingdom of God and his righteousness, and all these things will be added to you. Matthew 6:33 ESV

Lord, thank You, that You have the answers I need when it comes to educating my children. Remind me daily to come to You. Thank You for the opportunity to teach my children. Open my heart so I recognize what each of them need. Thank You, that Your help is always there and will never run dry. In Your name, Amen.

Further Reading: Matthew 6.

115

Musings on Being Content
Trudie Schar

Do you ever stop and think about contentment? Sometimes I find myself not content with this role as a homeschool mom. Not content with my life surrounded by kids, or lot in life with just one income. What about you?

Here are some musings I've been having. . .

- Being content is hardest when things around us are imperfect.
- Being content is learned.
- Being content is not found in looking at other people but in looking to God.
- Being content is seeing the big picture.
- Being content is seeing the lessons in the midst of the hard things.
- Being content is finding the little blessings in the midst of a hard climb.
- Being content is realizing the circumstances we are in right now, are preparing us, reshaping us, and strengthening our relationship with Jesus.
- Being content is hard.
- Being content starts with seeing with God's eyes.

SOME QUESTIONS I'VE BEEN ASKING MYSELF THIS YEAR. . .

Does being content come with things? A nice house? A new appliance? Wiggle room in the budget? Money?

Does it come with a good job? A perfect church? Lovely children? Romantic marriage?

Is contentment only for the good times? Is it for the vacations? The future? The happily ever after?

Is contentment only for the answered prayers? The Yes prayers... The ways that seem to all go smooth.

Or is contentment more than all that? Is being content for the hard times too?

Are we supposed to have a smooth life? Are we supposed to be content when things are going rough? Can we still enjoy life when things are going rough?

But godliness with contentment is great gain, for we brought nothing into the world, and we cannot take anything out of the world. But if we have food and clothing, with these we will be content. 1 Timothy 6:6-8 ESV

But godliness with contentment is great gain. For we brought nothing into this world, and it is certain we can carry nothing out. And having food and raiment let us be therewith content. 1 Timothy 6:6-8 KJV

Jesus, help me to be content even when things don't seem to be going good. Open my eyes to see the big picture, to see the ways that hard things bring me closer to You. Help me be content with the life you have in front of me. Not trying to run for the easy path, but help me stay and serve my people with contentment. This contentment only comes through You. Fill me up with it, I pray in Jesus' name. Amen.

Further Reading: 1 Timothy 6:6-12

116

A New Tool
Trudie Schar

The other day I got a trackpad for my iPad. It is basically a fancy mouse enabling me to work the iPad without having to reach out and touch the screen. My arm had been getting sore from reaching out to touch the screen, causing me headaches. This trackpad was going to help prevent that.

But. . . I've never used anything like it before. And of course, I've been reaching out my arm to touch the iPad screen for forever. (Like 6 years worth of forever.)

As I've been trying to get used to this new trackpad tool... there have been times that it is easier to just reach out my arm and use my finger. It's just easier. But the lesson I've been learning is, if I don't take the time to get used to the new tool I never will.

If I don't put in the hard work of breaking the old habit of reaching out to touch the screen I will never use the trackpad to its full advantage.

There are also things I never knew this trackpad could do until I read the manual. Swiping with two fingers can scroll a page. Swiping to the left with multiple fingers scrolls to another window. Cool things, that I never would have found without reading the manual.

If I don't learn all the ways to work it, I will never use it to its full potential.

All this made me think of homeschool curriculum. It is a tool. Sometimes in order to use it I have to let old habits die. It's hard to start something new... but if we never break those old habits, we won't be using the new curriculum or new tools to their full advantage.

Put in the hard work of breaking old habits.

Sometimes we need a bit of training to use the homeschool curriculum. I have quit using homeschool books because I didn't understand how to use them. In fact, the curriculum we use now is one that I said I would NEVER use. Why? Because I didn't understand how to get it to work. I used it for a year teaching private school, at the end of the year I found a lesson plan book. Inside the lesson plan book I found the KEY to teaching the curriculum. Funny, it's not as bad to use when you use it correctly.

Figure out how to use it correctly.

Homeschool curriculum is meant to be a tool — break the old habits and learn how to use it to its full potential.

For I know the plans I have for you, declares the Lord, plans for welfare[b] and not for evil, to give you a future and a hope. Jeremiah 29:11 ESV

For I know the thoughts that I think toward you, saith the Lord, thoughts of peace, and not of evil, to give you an expected end. Jeremiah 29:11 KJV

Jesus, thank You for the tools you have given me. Help me to break old habits so that I can fully use the tools I have. Help me dig in and learn how they were designed to be used. Show me how to use them to their full potential. If I need to change curriculum make that clear too. In Jesus' name, Amen.

Further Reading: Jeremiah 29:10-14

117

It's Not About Curriculum
Brittney Morris

Every new person who comes to the homeschooling fork in the road has 1 million questions. It never fails, the person they ask is the one and only homeschool mom they know. Me. The first question is always, "What's the best curriculum?"

I can surely give you recommendations. I can tell you the whole gambit of curriculums we've tried. But at the end of the day, the answer I really want to give them is this:

It's not about the curriculum. It's not about if your kids learn Latin by the time they go to middle school. It's not about being the winner of the homeschoolers spelling bee (I'm sure that's probably a thing?). It's not even about learning to do basic math (the old school way…not that "new math"!).

It's about relationships. It's about cultivating their hearts. It's about your heart, dear mama!

You can buy the most expensive program out there for your sweet kiddos, but at the end of the day, if we aren't pointing them towards Jesus, then what is even the point? God, as Creator of all the things we could ever learn anyways, is at the very center of every math problem, book, and science experiment.

Numbers reveal His order. Art reveals His creativity. Science reveals His intentional planning.

It's not about the curriculum. Take them outside and observe what God has created. Talk about how only God could create a butterfly. Listen to great classical music. Talk about how God sings loudly over His people. Play a game of basketball. Talk about how God has fearfully and wonderfully created each of us.

You see, when we know our Creator, and we understand that He, indeed, is the Creator of all things, we have an invitation to explore learning in a whole new way. We are invited to search for the mark of the Creator in all things.

As we begin to search out our Creator with our children, an opportunity is born for us to not only cultivate their hearts for Jesus, but also to build a relationship with them ourselves. The biggest blessing of homeschooling is the ability to learn about our Savior with our children, to have tender moments that show them we are humans looking for answers too. To offer the gentle answer, and to have quality time together.

No greater gifts could any boxed curriculum afford you. Take the time to just be. Be together. Be learners. Be seekers. Be still.

All things were made through Him, and without Him was not anything made that was made.
John 1:3 ESV

All things were made by Him; and without Him was not any thing made that was made.
John 1:3 KJV

Dear Jesus, You were present at creation. By Your hand the foundations of the earth were laid. Galaxies hold their places, earth spins, and waters remain in their boundaries, at Your command. When my heart is overwhelmed with what my children "ought to know," take me by the hand and gently lead me back to You. Remind me that the most important thing to teach my children is of Your great love and Your unending grace. You are the Creator of all things, Lord; help me to seek You in each lesson throughout our school day. In Jesus' name, Amen.

Further Reading: Psalm 61:1-4

118

Seeing Things Through His Eyes
Trudie Schar

A couple of days ago we read about contentment. How's it going? You know, sometimes I think the key to being content is seeing the situation through the eyes of Jesus.

When we see through the eyes of Jesus we see that:

- Hard things bring us closer to Him.
- Hard things cause us to lean on His strength, rather than our own.
- Hard things make our muscles increase.
- The BIG Picture. Not just the little situation we have right before us.
- How wicked our heart can be, how the tough things make us ooze with complaints, worries, and discontent. Seeing our heart we realize how much we need a Savior to rescue us from the doubt we feel. To rescue us from the sin we get so easily distracted by.
- How loved we are. We can see how the hard things actually form us into the person Christ wants us to be. The hard things make us into someone who is able to help others in the same situations. It makes us realize that these hard things we are going through are not because God doesn't love us, but rather that He is refining us.

Seeing through the eyes of **Jesus**

Seeing through the Eyes of Jesus; means remembering His past faithfulness and trusting Him to carry us through whatever is in front of us.

Being content is just that; looking at the big picture and seeing what God has in mind with what we are going through just this very minute. Good and bad. That we see the hard things that come in our life OR the hard things that STAY in our life, that we can't get over; as exercises to make us into who we are created to be. Remembering how He has been faithful and being content knowing that He is still faithful.

Not that I am speaking of being in need, for I have learned in whatever situation I am to be content. I know how to be brought low, and I know how to abound. In any and every circumstance, I have learned the secret of facing plenty and hunger, abundance and need. I can do all things through him who strengthens me. Philippians 4:11-13 ESV

Not that I speak in respect of want: for I have learned, in whatsoever state I am, therewith to be content. I know both how to be abased, and I know how to abound: everywhere and in all things I am instructed both to be full and to be hungry, both to abound and to suffer need. I can do all things through Christ which strengtheneth me. Philippians 4:11-13 KJV

Jesus, teach me to be content. That in whatever state I am I can see how You are right beside me. That even when I suffer You are beside me. That I can get through it, I can be content even when I'm going through something tough. Help me through this school year. That I can be content through it. In Jesus' name, Amen.

Further Reading: Philippians 4:11-13

119

Exploring Creation
Karen Geiser

One of the most treasured shelves on our homeschool bookshelf holds our vast collection of nature field guides. Most were gifts from grandparents and relatives, some are well tattered, many are used frequently. Living on a farm, it is a natural part of our homeschooling to let our children explore God's amazing Creation and the many plants, flowers and creatures that are around us. Looking closely into the hidden things of God gives us a deeper appreciation for how He intricately wove all of Creation to work together. Like Solomon who described plants and animals, I want to encourage my children to discover things in depth and be able to share them with others.

He (Solomon) spoke of trees, from the cedar that is in Lebanon to the hyssop that grow out of the wall. He spoke also of beasts, and of birds, and of reptiles, and of fish. I Kings 4:33 ESV

And he (Solomon) spake of trees, from the cedar tree that is in Lebanon even unto the hyssop that springeth out of the wall; he spake also of beasts, and of fowl, and of creeping things, and of fishes. I Kings 4:33 KJV

The field guides have helped us identify many strange bugs, unknown tree leaves, migrating birds who are with us for just a brief moment and unique wildflowers. My children use the guides to quiz each other on bird species and to ask their mother if she knows the adult weight of a Himalayan three toed woodpecker. We draw things in nature journals, press leaves and I find items like bugs in the freezer, rocks on the kitchen table and feathers on the piano (all waiting to be identified, of course.) The guides have also given some of my children a longing to travel to exotic rain forests in search of colorful flora and fauna. Nature books are definitely an investment worth making and are an excellent gift giving idea.

"There's not a plant or flower below but makes thy glory known." (from the hymn I Sing the Mighty Power of God)

The study of nature is quite popular among homeschoolers and people in general, coming from all flavors of faith convictions. It encompasses everyone from tree huggers to staunch creationists. Don't stop at just learning the details, intentionally make your nature study point to a wonderful Creator whose design skills are par excellence. Connect your children with the Creator's greatest field guide, the Bible, as you search for references to plants, animals, sky and more.

There's not a plant or flower below but makes

thy **glory** known.

Dear Lord, I stand amazed at the details of Your Creation. Help me to encourage my children to search out the hidden things that you have created. As they learn more about what you have made, may they also desire to learn more about the Maker.

In Jesus' name, Amen.

Further Reading: Psalm 104:24-30

120

Giving Mercy
Trudie Schar

I'm not sure what started the spat. This mom's brain can't remember. Yet, I think you can get the picture; the conversation went something like this... Yelling loudly, the big sister said, "Mooommmm, SHE is on the IPad and she's not supposed to be."

I responded with a "Ok, what should her punishment be; if she's doing something when it is not the right time? Doing something when she's not supposed to be?"

Big sister listed off a whole pile of punishments. They were not easy things. The list included things like no iPad time tomorrow, clean the whole basement, and sit on a chair.

Ouch.

Never-the-less I wrote the whole list on the board. Next, I asked her, "Now, I have a question for you. What are YOU supposed to be doing?"

Oh, she knew she was caught. She looked at the floor and mumbled, "School"

"School. Hummm, what were you doing instead?"

"Playing," was her humble response.

The conversation went on, I said, "Ok, so, that whole list that you have for your sister to do... you really listed it off for yourself to do? YOU are not doing what you are supposed to do, just like your sister wasn't. Hummm, maybe I should have you do that list of punishments too!"

That stopped the accusations right in its track.

My little gal, she knew her sister deserved that list of punishments, yet all of a sudden she realized she deserved them too.

Have you ever been there before? Dished out a list of punishments that another mom or friend deserved, and then realized that YOU deserved the very same punishment.
Mercy.

Mercy is easy to give yourself. Harder to give to others.

Mercy is the withholding of punishment. It is forgiving even when we are in the wrong.

We are all sinners. We all have a list of punishments we deserve. Yet Jesus, He gives mercy every time.

Every. Time.

For the Lord is good; his steadfast love endures forever, and his faithfulness to all generations.
Psalm 100:5 ESV

For the Lord is good; his mercy is everlasting; and his truth endureth to all generations.
Psalm 100:5 KJV

Lord, help me rest in Your mercy! Help me extend Your mercy to each other. In Jesus' Name I pray, Amen.

Further Reading: Psalm 100

121

Our Kids Our Not Our Own
Trudie Schar

Recently we were looking into getting a puppy. We found one we liked, he was a cute little guy.

Here's what might happen next. We would decide, yep this is the one for us. We would pay the guy a deposit.

But it's not time for us to pick him up yet. Is the puppy ours or not?
The puppy legally would be ours . . . But still in the care of the seller.

The seller would need to decide, how does he treat a dog that is NOT his? I wonder if he would:

- treat it at arm's length so he does not get attached
- get attached and be preparing for hurt when he leaves.
- be annoyed every time he takes care of it. Muttering under his breath
- be nervous and paranoid that he's going to die/ruin it
- be visibly mad at it. Kicking etc.

Our kids are not our OWN.

Friend, our kids are not our own. They have a deposit on them. They are really God's. We are just taking care of them for a little season. We have the same options as that dog seller does.

How are we going to treat these precious children that are really not ours?

"Suffer the little children to come unto me, and forbid them not: for of such is the kingdom of God." Mark 10:14 ESV

Suffer the little children to come unto me, and forbid them not: for of such is the kingdom of God. Mark 10:14 KJV

Jesus, my children really are not mine. Help me to take care of them the way You would take care of them. Not grudgingly or with anger. Not keeping an arms length to protect my heart from pain when they leave. Show me how to love and care for them as I am caring for your children. Because that is who they are. In Your name I pray, Amen.

Further Reading: Mark 10:13-16

122

Patiently Listening
Phyllis Keith Boles

Discouragement meets me at the foot of my bed this morning.

I'm not expecting her. But after yesterday, maybe I am.

She clings to me as I wash, get dressed and plunge down the stairs to start my day.

She tries to grab my heart to become angry at the books that are sprawled on the kitchen floor.

She tries to pull me past my morning meeting place with God. But I am not having it.

I sit down in my usual chair for my devotion. I read the words in my Bible.

I don't speak.

I just listen to what the Lord is saying to me from the pages of scripture.

Thankfully, I obey the voice of God not to follow discouragement into my day. She will not win. Not like she did yesterday. Ugh, I don't want to fight with my children today. Yesterday, my children ignored these words. "Please, finish your chores in the next 15 minutes." "Do you understand this math concept? If not, I am willing to go over it with you until you understand it."

As I sit quietly in my devotion time, I focus on the verse,

> "The Lord will fight for you, and you have only to be silent." Exodus 14:14 ESV

> "The Lord shall fight for you, and ye shall hold your peace." Exodus 14:14 KJV

Listening to God's voice, other voices, and even our own thoughts, require critical aspects of attention, understanding, and discernment. Because listening takes on the process of filtering the information we receive, it becomes more effective than our speech. The baby in the womb enters this world after hearing conversations for months. As babies grow into the childhood years, they are trained to respond to what they hear. And for the elderly, speech has quelled almost to a silence as they yearn to hear a voice of comfort during the long days of silence. From the beginning of the baby's existence to the end of the elderly's existence, God has instilled in them the beauty of listening.

In your homeschool day, One voice reigns over all other voices. The voices of your children, the voices of curriculum choices, or the voices telling you to give up must bow down to God's whispers. Be still. Lean close to Him. Don't give up. Keep teaching your children. Listening is a skill developed over the years. Remember you are imparting words of life they will always remember.

Lord, I know I am not good at listening. It has taken years for me to be able to listen well. Father, you always listen to my prayers. You hear me when I call. You even know what I need before I even ask. You are amazingly patient with me. Please help me to be patient with my children when it seems they are not listening to you or to me. Quiet me and my children to hear what is good and right. In Jesus' name, Amen.

Further Reading: Proverbs 19:20, Psalm 116:1-2, Romans 10:17

123

Be Strong and Courageous
Trudie Schar

Are you worried about all the littles God has placed in your life? Do you worry you are inadequate to lead them?

There was a man who had people to lead, and he felt inadequate. They were not his children, but God's chosen nation. This man, Joshua, had cities and lands to conquer. He had problems on every side.

Take a moment and read Joshua 1 today. You will read that Joshua was chosen to lead the Israelites into the promised land after Moses died. Listen to the words Moses told Joshua over and over to encourage him in the calling;

"Have I not commanded you? Be strong and courageous. Do not be frightened, and do not be dismayed, for the Lord your God is with you wherever you go." Joshua 1:9 ESV

Have not I commanded thee? Be strong and of a good courage; be not afraid, neither be thou dismayed: for the Lord thy God is with thee whithersoever thou goest. Joshua 1:9 KJV

Do you feel inadequate to teach your children? To homeschool? To lead them?

God says the same to you;
Sweet Mama, Be STRONG and COURAGEOUS! For you are the one to lead these little people. Study the Bible, meditate on it night and day. Do not be afraid or discouraged. Look to Jesus!

Jesus, thank You for this reminder to not be afraid. Sometimes the task is daunting and I get overwhelmed. Fill me with strength and courage. Help me teach, lead, guide my children today. I look to You for my help. In Jesus' name, Amen.

Read Joshua 1:1-18

Be strong and courageous

124

The Journey
Tabatha Slater

My husband and I were stuck in China. We were waiting to bring our daughter back home to America with us. We had gone about the adoption process the wrong way and the Chinese authorities were not happy that their rules had not been followed.

We lived in China. God miraculously placed our daughter into our family, but the adoption was not going well. We were prepared to stay in China for as long as we had to, yet we had no idea how long that would be.

I drew comfort from the story in the Book of Numbers when the Israelites were wandering in the desert. They did not know how long they would be there. Yet, they had a clear visual to follow, a cloud during the day and a pillar of fire at night.

Can you imagine not knowing when you would leave? Two days? A month? A YEAR?

The Israelites were eagerly awaiting their arrival to Canaan. They had to wait on God to direct their path. God was there, He was communicating with them through Moses, clouds, and fire. He provided by giving them mana to eat and cared for them even though they grumbled and complained.

In China we were asking God similar questions like, "How long before we can go home Lord? Two days? A month? A YEAR?" His answer was two and a half years. God provided while we were there.

When we began homeschooling, we took a similar approach, one school year at a time. Again, we asked, "How long will we be doing this Lord?" His answer, more than 20 years so far.

Maybe you have been thrown into homeschooling unexpectedly.

This time of uncertainty is your "wilderness."

Perhaps you're wondering if you can do this, or maybe how LONG you can do this. You can do this, dear sister! God will provide, God will take care of you. The Holy Spirit will direct your path.

May you find great joy through walking in obedience, trusting our caring God along the way! The road will be hard, there will be many obstacles, we may grumble and complain, but our Lord will be walking beside you all the way.

Whether it was two days, or a month, or a longer time, that the cloud continued over the tabernacle, abiding there, the people of Israel remained in camp and did not set out, but when it lifted they set out. Numbers 9:22 ESV

Father, thank you that you are here, walking beside me on my homeschooling journey. You are my refuge and my strength. You will never leave me or forsake me. Help me to remember to put my trust in you during this time of uncertainty. May I follow your leading in our homeschool and allow you to direct my path. In Jesus' name I pray. Amen.

Further Reading : Numbers 9

125

Have You Asked?
Trudie Schar

Something hit me the other day. Here are the verses I read:

What causes quarrels and what causes fights among you? Is it not this, that your passions are at war within you? You desire and do not have, so you murder. You covet and cannot obtain, so you fight and quarrel. You do not have, because you do not ask. You ask and do not receive, because you ask wrongly, to spend it on your passions. James 4:1-3 ESV

From whence come wars and fightings among you? Come they not hence, even of your lusts that war in your members? Ye lust, and have not: ye kill, and desire to have, and cannot obtain: ye fight and war, yet ye have not, because ye ask not. Ye ask, and receive not, because ye ask amiss, that ye may consume it upon your lusts. James 4:1-3 KJV

James says they were fighting and lusting and wishing after things for their own benefit. So they could advance their own purpose.

But what really stuck out to me is that part of verse 3 " You have not because you ask not"

What have you been wanting? Have you asked for it? Have you taken it to God in prayer?

Another question. . . Why do you want it? Why do you desire it so much?
At times I've wanted something good — peace in our homeschool. But my reason is quite selfish. Sigh.

I've wanted my kids to stop fighting or to have an easy day. Again, my reason is selfish.

But just think what would happen if I asked. . . For peace in my homeschool with the purpose of bringing God more glory. Or sharing His name. Or so the environment of our homeschool would be one in which my kids would be able to thrive. Just think of the results of asking inside God's purpose!

I'm reminded to ask. I have not because I ask not.

Jesus, I'm sorry when I have selfishly asked for things. Help me desire things for the right reason. Remind me to ask. I have not because I don't ask. Sometimes I don't ask because I lack faith, please increase my faith. In Jesus' name, Amen.

Further Reading: James 4:1-10

126

My Inabilities
Trudie Schar

Do you ever step back and stare at a day . . . Wondering how you will ever make it to bedtime? Or stare at the lesson plans for the next week and wonder how you will get to Friday?

Ugh. Me too.

My list of inabilities is large. It seems with each thing I do learn, there are another two to add to the list of things that I don't know how to do.

Then I remember Jesus.

Jesus is able.

I've heard the quote repeated "If God calls you to it, He will make a way." Yes, that is true. Yet it doesn't happen the way I first imagined it.

When God called me to homeschool He knew I was unable to do it. I would have thought that His way of "making a way" would be to enable me to do it. Myself. Like magically creating me to be patient and loving. Magically make me a teacher who explains things clearly. Magically makes me full of energy to conquer everything.

I thought He would make me ABLE to do it myself.

Yes, He makes a way . . . But not through my own abilities.

He makes a way by LEANING into His power.

Perhaps, if He would make me able, I would trust in my own abilities. However, He is wise and doesn't do that. Rather, He proves Himself able to provide for me.

Friend, what looks daunting today? He is able to make a way. Lean into HIS power.

Fear not, for I am with you; be not dismayed, for I am your God; I will strengthen you, I will help you, I will uphold you with my righteous right hand. Isaiah 41:10 ESV

Fear thou not; for I am with thee: be not dismayed; for I am thy God: I will strengthen thee; yea, I will help thee; yea, I will uphold thee with the right hand of my righteousness. Isaiah 41:10 KJV

Jesus, You have called me to something I'm not able to do on my own. I need Your power. I can't do this by myself. I plead with You, please come beside me and do the impossible. I praise You for giving me strength for this large task. In Your name I pray, Amen.

Further Reading: Isaiah 41:8-14

127

Keep Pressing On, Mama
Danielle Hope Poorman

I held my breath as the irrepressible urge to heave the books across the room overcame me. Drowning in lesson plans, dishes, laundry, and writing deadlines, I convinced myself that homeschooling was a mistake. I didn't feel qualified to instruct my children in Latin or Algebraic equations.

Have you ever felt this way?

We all have those days where weariness takes over and leaves us with seeds of doubt in our calling. Mama, let me encourage you that although you may not feel "equipped" to teach your children, you are the best teacher for the job.

We are not perfect people, and we are going to FAIL. Our children need to see that. When that happens, they can witness the beautiful redemption of grace that accompanies the failure.

Our failures are not a surprise to God. As parents, we guide our children to truth in all areas of life.

Why?

Because God has called us too. That is why we keep going. We are called.

In Deuteronomy, God instructs the Israelites to teach their children from the time they rise until they go to bed (Deuteronomy 11). This command goes far beyond academic instruction. As parents, we're called to teach and display the character of God to our children. In our weak moments, the enemy discourages us in thinking that is a daunting task! However, God has equipped us with His precious Word and His strength that enables us to do so. The God who walked with the Israelites through the wilderness will surely walk with us on this homeschooling journey!

The apostle Paul writes, "He who began a good work in you will bring it to completion at the day of Jesus Christ" (Philippians 1:6). The Lord has called us to homeschool our precious children, and He has also promised to equip us with everything we need. His grace is sufficient for today and tomorrow.

So, keep pressing on and pressing upward, Mama! The God who has called you to homeschooling will help you complete it.

Therefore, my beloved brothers, be steadfast, immovable, always abounding in the work of the Lord, knowing that in the Lord your labor is not in vain. I Corinthians 15:58 ESV

Therefore, my beloved brethren, be ye steadfast, unmovable, always abounding in the work of the Lord, forasmuch as ye know that your labour is not in vain in the Lord.
I Corinthians 15:58 KJV

Jesus, I know you have called me to this wonderful work of homeschooling. Please help me to seek You daily for the strength I need to accomplish the work You have for me. Let my daily faithfulness to Your calling be a shining light to my children. Hold me fast and grant me Your grace to keep pressing on for Your honor and glory. In Jesus' name, Amen.

Further Reading: 1 Corinthians 15:

128

The Benefits of Exercise
Trudie Schar

Have your kids been kinda sleepy or lackadaisical during school lately? Maybe they just haven't been able to concentrate or sit still?

Something I heard recently BLEW my mind! The speaker said that when a kid exercises they get extra oxygen flowing to the brain. . . Ready for it?? TWO hours worth of extra oxygen.

When I went and researched it I found phrases like

- Increased short term memory
- Faster reaction time
- Higher level of creativity
- Increased openness to learning
- Higher capacity for knowledge
- Aids in maintaining attention
- Better ability to coordinate action and thoughts crisply
- Increases ability to learn
- Increases mental awareness
- Decreases stress

WHEW! That is quite the list. I need some of these benefits in my life. . . And my kids sure do too!

And I wonder why is exercise an afterthought to me?!

For while bodily training is of some value, godliness is of value in every way, as it holds promise for the present life and also for the life to come. 1 TImothy 4:8 ESV

For bodily exercise profiteth little: but godliness is profitable unto all things, having promise of the life that now is, and of that which is to come. 1 Timothy 4:8 KJV

Previously when I read this verse I thought, "Oh exercise is not important. . . Godliness is." BUT today it looks differently. Think of ALL the benefits of exercise that I discovered; science proves there are so many benefits! And just think the Bible just says they are "some value"! Imagine how much more the benefits of Godliness are!

Jesus, thank You for this knowledge of how much exercise benefits us. Help me keep this on my mind as I go through the day; but for me and my kids. Give us the motivation to exercise so we can take advantage of the many benefits. It blows my mind how much it can help us, but even more so how much Godliness is above exercise. Show us how to add Godliness to our lives. In Jesus' name, Amen.

Further Reading: 1 Timothy 4:6-9

129

His Wondrous Works
Barb Schwind

Our 3 year old granddaughter, Elsie, was looking through a Bible storybook when she came across a picture of the stone rolled in front of the tomb. "Oh no, they are trapping God! She called out."

She turned the page, "Oh, He got out again!"

She was truly involved in the wonder of the story.

Am I Amazed?

Am I amazed in my daily devotions at the stories in the Bible and the teachings in the Word? Do I sing hymns with the enthusiasm my little ones show?

Life gets so very busy - teaching, caring for children, cleaning, cooking, laundry, business, yard work, entertaining, volunteering and the list goes on. Sometimes reading the Bible becomes another thing to check off my to do list for the day.

At times I get distracted by the cares or trials of life.

Lord, I don't want it to be that way. I want to be amazed at how you work in the lives of men and women of the Bible and I want to soak in and apply your teachings. Help us to learn and praise You with an enthusiastic heart like we often see in our children and grandchildren.

Although we take on the role of teacher we can learn much from our little ones, too!

"I will remember the deeds of the Lord, yes, I will remember your wonders of old."
Psalm 77:11 ESV

"I will remember the works of the Lord, surely I will remember thy wonders of old."
Psalm 77:11 KJV

Lord, thank You for placing these little ones in my life who show enthusiasm for the stories found in Your Word and for songs of praise to You. Lord, help me have a childlike heart who worships my Heavenly Father with joy and exuberance. Bring to my mind the many wonders You have done not only for Bible characters but also for me and those I love. In Jesus' name. Amen.

Further Reading: Psalm 77:11-14

130

Praying for the Little Things
Trudie Schar

It seems silly. But sometimes I pray the oddest things for my children.

Things like finding a "friend in church", understanding a certain math concept, an owie to heal, and being able to sleep at night.

We tend to pray about all kinds of little things. Maybe it's a little silly. But I've seen them becoming prayer warriors.

They have people on their list that they pray for every night. (Each meal too). When we hear news of someone being sick, they stop what they are doing and pray.

Praying over little things teaches them to pray over the big things.

What about you, sweet homeschool mom? Have you been praying for the little things for yourself? Things like patience to get through that spelling test or listening to your 1st grader slowly read again. Things like energy to wash the table off after the last snack. Or a new curriculum when your current one is not working. Have you been praying for the little things?

God cares about your little things. He wants a relationship with you. He wants to have conversations with you. He wants you to talk to Him about anything.

Pray for the little things.

Pray without ceasing. 1 Thessalonians 5:13 ESV

Pray without ceasing. 1 Thessalonians 5:13 KJV

Jesus, sometimes I feel silly praying for the little things. Give me strength when I am tired. Help me have patience when school is taking a while. Fill me with peace even when my mind is so full. Show up in my life. Thank you for listening and caring when I tell You everything that is on my mind. In Your name I pray, Amen.

Read 1 Thessalonians 5:12-22

Pray without ceasing

131

Roots of Hurt and Blame
Angel Lambert

Behold, I have refined you, but not as silver; I have tried you in the furnace of affliction.
Isaiah 48:10 ESV

Behold, I have refined thee, but not with silver; I have chosen thee in the furnace of affliction.
Isaiah 48:10 KJV

This school year, I will learn to repent of the bitterness and resentment I feel creeping up into my heart. My children do not listen or obey quickly, quietly, and cheerfully. They balk at doing the work I set before them. They do not come when I call, get ready when instructed, or complete the tasks I give them. Sound familiar? I am certain God feels this way about me.

Repentance is the answer.

There is no room in a believer's heart for stagnation and hatred.

Maybe you are home educating in unhappy circumstances. Perhaps it was not your first choice, or your second, third, or fifteenth. But here you are, walking this path. There may be bitterness and resentment in your heart as well, with roots of complaint, dissatisfaction, and blame growing gnarled, thorny weeds as you walk along. These hurts in your heart can paralyze and keep you stuck, strangling out the good you could be planting in your children's hearts.

The Lord will forgive every hard spot in our hearts, every hurtful rebellious thought, and every fist which clenches around the disappointments we fold into it. He will cleanse every corner of our souls and dig out this evil to destroy it. The coming year may be difficult and painful for me and you, but I am confident that every trial He allows for us and pulls us through only refines us into lovely, precious works of silver art. As terrifying as the unknown appears, and as uncertain as I am about the proving grounds, I have no doubt whatsoever that the end results will be entirely worth all of it.

You will cleanse me. 1 John 1:9

You will refine me through fire. 1 Peter 1:6-8, Zechariah 13:9

You will send me on missions, even in my own home. Matthew 4:19

You will bring me back into the fold as a leader, not of others but as one who points the way to you through servanthood and caring. Matthew 23:10, Luke 22:26

You will also convince me of kindness, not because I need a reason but because I have forgotten how. Romans 11:22, 2 Samuel 2:6, Ephesians 4:32, Colossians 3: 12-13

You will bring mercy into my life. Micah 6:8

So, Lord, here are my goals for this year; I hand them to You. But no matter what I plan, I want to give myself up to be planted in Your garden. Help me do as You ask. Give me courage to be bold. Remind me to be gentle. Teach me to forgive, repent, run to You, and show mercy, both to others and myself. Lord, bring me to Your joy. In Jesus' name, Amen.

132

There's Not Just One Right Way
Trudie Schar

When I began homeschooling I thought there was only ONE right way.

You know, like folding towels. There is only one way to do it right. Only one way to do laundry. Only one way to menu plan. Oh yes, one way to dress too. (Especially if you are a homeschooler. So they say LOL)

So when I found differences in homeschooling, of course, I thought one of us was wrong. And I'm pretty sure it wasn't me. 😏

I even had a couple of ideas for my own homeschool. Things that I truly thought I would NEVER do! Like use a certain curriculum and use a certain method. It's not real homeschooling I SAID.OUT.LOUD.

And then . . . God laid on my heart to use said curriculum and use said media method. So now, clearly, I am doing it all wrong.

You know, that is when I realized that neither of us are wrong. That is when I realized that God designed us to all be different.

Neither of us are wrong

Just as He created us each to look different. He never meant for our homeschool to look the same. There is NOT just one right way for ALL of us. But for ALL of us there is a right way. And we can not compare our "right way" with each other.

Are you ever tempted to compare your homeschool with someone else's? Don't do it. God never meant for us to look like them.

I praise you, for I am fearfully and wonderfully made. Wonderful are your works; my soul knows it very well. Psalm 139:14 ESV

I will praise thee; for I am fearfully and wonderfully made: marvellous are thy works; and that my soul knoweth right well. Psalm 139:14 KJV

Jesus, thank You for the reminder that my homeschool is not supposed to look like anyone else's. Help me to avoid comparing myself with others. Show me how You want our homeschool to look. Then give me the grace to accomplish it. In Your name I pray, Amen.

Further Reading: Psalm 139:13-18

In the Garden
Karen Geiser

The gardens on our farm are ripe with lessons for school and life. Our children join us in planting, weeding and harvesting. Biology abounds as we work at balancing soil nutrients, observe both beneficial and pesky insects, plant unique plant specimens and learn about pollinators. Plus, the children are learning to navigate business transactions as they sell produce they raised. There are joys such as the first ripe tomato or blooming tulip, as well as disappointments of rabbits eating lettuce to the quick or a storm flattening the corn

Gardens are a fabulous medium for homeschooling, whether you can plant a large one like ours or just a small pot on the windowsill or porch. So many life lessons await and the fringe benefit of food, flowers or herbs is a bonus.

Gardens play a significant role in the Bible as well.

Life on earth began in a garden (Eden), Jesus spent a final agonizing night in a garden (Gethsemane) and a future garden is described in Revelation (New Jerusalem.) Jesus frequently shared object lessons and parables using garden terminology and observations. His audience was agrarian and He spoke in symbols they could connect with, but sometimes those things aren't part of our modern culture. Sowing seeds and tending plants as part of school doesn't just produce green beans, it can lead to a deeper understanding of God's Word. Seeing how good soil and rocky soil differ, witnessing weeds choke out the good plants, observing how tiny a mustard seed is and helping prune a grape vine can all give insight to the meanings of Jesus' stories.

Garden object lessons are also significant for us as parents. We want to cultivate our children's hearts so the soil is rich and fertile and God's Word can grow abundantly in them. What are we doing to intentionally make that happen during our school time and our daily routines? Make sure your lesson plan includes planting seeds, both the physical and spiritual kind, and watch your homeschool grow and flourish.

Still other seed fell on good soil, where it produced a crop – a hundred, sixty or thirty times what was sown. Matthew 13:8 ESV

But other fell into good ground, and brought forth fruit, some an hundredfold, some sixty fold, some thirtyfold. Matthew 13: 8 KJV

Dear Lord, I thank you for the gift of gardens, large and small. Help our families to understand your Word on a deeper level as we experience planting and tending a garden first hand. May the soil of our hearts be prepared for the seeds you want to plant in each of us. In Jesus' name, Amen.

Further Reading: Matthew 13:1-9

134

A Recovering Kid Pleaser
Trudie Schar

You've heard of a "people pleaser," right?

It's when you going about life always trying to please people. You say "yes" even when you'd rather say "no." It's when you tiptoe around issues because you don't want to rock the boat. Or when you are afraid of showing someone your true self, because you are afraid of rejection. It's when you are out just to impress someone else.

You are out to "please people."

Have you been there, done that? It's ok, this is a safe place to admit you've done it too.

In some ways, it is not bad to be polite and kind. But when it gets between us and what God has for us people pleasing has gone too far.

> For do I now persuade men, or God? or do I seek to please men? for if I yet pleased men, I should not be the servant of Christ. Galatians 1:10 ESV

> For do I now persuade men, or God? or do I seek to please men? for if I yet pleased men, I should not be the servant of Christ. Galatians 1:10 KJV

Did you know your kids can fall into this "people" category.

Sometimes as moms we fall into this "Kid Pleasing." It looks a little like saying "yes" even when your gut says the answer should be "no." It looks like tiptoeing around making rules and boundaries because you don't want to be mean. It looks like not putting your foot down on an issue because you don't want to deal with the blow up that is about to happen. It is trying to do everything for your kids, so there is no rejection. It is trying to be sure they like you.

It's people pleasing. And it's wrong.

We are not the "mom" to make everyone happy. We are the mom to be the mom. We are here to train and teach our children. God wants us to be merciful and kind, yes! But He also wants us to set rules, guidelines, and boundaries.

We are here to please God. And He wants us to point our kids to Jesus. Not to make them happy with us.

Is there something you need to put your foot down on? Is there an area where you've been trying to "kid please"? Please God, homeschool mama, He is the One we are living for.

Jesus, there are times that I fall into the trap of pleasing my kids. I want them to be happy. I want to be a good mom in their eyes. Yet I know that they need guidelines and boundaries. I know they need to learn what is right and wrong. I know they need to learn how to do chores and be responsible. Help me know how to train them to please YOU. Give me strength to put my foot down when I need to, without fear of rejection. Lead me. In Jesus' name, Amen.

Further Reading: Galatians 1:6-10

135

I Am Complete When We Are Together
Darcy Schock

I try so hard. Yet, often it never feels like it is enough. Comparison sets in and I begin analyzing my skills. I compare my homeschool to public school. I wonder if the bad days will overshadow the good. When it comes down to it as hard as I try to be enough, I never make it. The reality that I am lacking big time can weigh heavy on me.

It is natural to talk about striving to be more like Jesus, to shine His love. That's my deep desire. My main goal during homeschool is that my kids can see Jesus' love shine through me. That I am a reflection of Him always.

But what about when I am not? What about when I fall short of showing His perfect love? Have I failed? Is all lost? Should I stop trying to be enough when I am aware that I will never be fully enough--no matter how hard I try?

I am sure you have heard it said, "Give God your best and He will do the rest. God will fill in the gaps." What does that look like when I mess up? How does it practically play out in my life each day?

For too long I have lived like this: I will work really hard then hope and pray God covers what I can't do. I will do my part and hope God picks up the slack. But I think that is the wrong way to look at it.

Me and Him, we are a team. It is Us. I am not called to take all the burdens on myself then leave God the leftovers. When I take the burdens on myself and pray He picks up the slack, unhealthy stuff creeps in. I begin to falsely believe that if I try hard enough I may be complete and if not, I have let Him down.

Matthew 11:29-30 says: "Take my yoke upon you, and learn of me; for I am meek and lowly in heart: and ye shall find rest unto your souls. For my yoke is easy, and my burden is light."

KJV

"Take my yoke upon you, and learn from me, for I am gentle and lowly in heart, and you will find rest for your souls. For my yoke is easy, and my burden is light." Matthew 11:29-30 ESV

For My yoke is easy and My burden is light

— Jesus

We weren't meant to carry the burden of homeschool alone and pray Jesus picks up the slack. We were meant to team with Him. Him in me and me in Him. Where I am weak, He is strong. Where I am unable, He is able. It's running hand in hand, not passing the baton. I am not so sure it is simply "He fills in the gaps" or "I do my best and leave Him the rest". Maybe more accurately it is: I am complete when we are together.

Lord Jesus teach me how to take your yoke so we can pull together as a team. I want to abide in You and You in me so there is no separation; only together. Help me lay down my burdens and trust You. Make me complete. Fill in the void of "not enough" with You. Please be what I can't be in our homeschool. In Jesus' name, Amen.

Further Reading: John 15:4-11

136

We Lead Gently Because He Gently Leads
Tandy Sue Hogate

School Work

Chores

Math Camp

Dentist Appointment

Geography Bee Rehearsal

History Co-Op

Homeschool Soccer Practice

Awana

Does this look like a typical day on your calendar? Fitting everything in is just plain exhausting.

I remember the homeschool days of old when we had very few outside opportunities. Our days were full and busy but not overly stressful. There was plenty of time for essential lessons beyond school, like habit forming, Bible reading, and gently handling matters of the heart.

By the time our older three kids were in middle school, we started adding more into our day. First, it was Awana, and piano. Next, we added daily track practice. Then some friends and I started a local homeschool co-op. But we didn't stop there. I took on a part-time job with a national magazine, my daughter started taking horse riding lessons, and my boys each got jobs.

Our sweet days turned chaotic. And the peaceful rhythm that had once reigned in our home slowly gave way to sloppy work and harsh words.

I recall one afternoon when I gained clarity on how we had gotten too busy. My daughter was struggling through her science class, a class she usually really looked forward to. But on this particular day, she couldn't seem to concentrate. My oldest son was also having a hard time completing his schoolwork. We had to leave at 1pm for track practice, followed by work, a horse lesson, then Awana.

But we were all falling apart.

My initial reaction was to get upset with them and push them harder. After all, the calendar said there was time for everything. So why were we getting farther and farther behind?

But God, in all His beautiful grace, reminded me of a passage I had read several years before.

He will tend his flock like a shepherd; he will gather the lambs in his arms;
he will carry them in his bosom, and gently lead those that are with young. Isaiah 40:11 ESV

He shall feed his flock like a shepherd: he shall gather the lambs with his arm, and carry them
in his bosom, and shall gently lead those that are with young. Isaiah 40:11 KJV

I read that verse repeatedly and prayed, begging God to show me where we had gone awry. I was not following His gentle leading. So, we canceled our afternoon plans, and I sat down with the kids and listened to their hearts. Through prayer, time in God's Word, and deep conversation, we saw how we needed to get our family back in the center of God's ever so kind will.

Jesus, we have so many amazing opportunities as homeschoolers, sometimes it can be hard to tell what we should be doing. Between home life, extracurricular activities, and church meetings, our lives can get busier than You intend. Help us to wisely seek Your guidance and trust that You are directing us in the way everlasting. In Jesus' name, Amen.

For further encouragement, I encourage you to dwell on Psalm 57.

137

Homeschool Success
Trudie Schar

What does success look like for you?

I'm not talking about book contracts or job promotions. I'm talking about your homeschool. What does success in your homeschool look like?

Is it checking all the boxes?
Is it getting 100% on the tests?
Is it getting done before noon?

Or is it. . .

Teaching your kids to be responsible and finish their chores.
Introducing your children to Jesus and the Bible.
Learning to get along and work together as a family.

What is **success** to you?

What is success to you?

My next question is. . . Does your "everyday" routine point towards your vision of success?

If success is to raise children who are responsible . . . Are you giving them responsibilities to practice with?

If success is to introduce your children to Jesus. . . Are you reading the Bible? Are you studying with them?

If success is to get along and work together as a family . . . Are you teaching them to work through differences and misunderstandings?

I love this verse:

> Where there is no prophetic vision the people cast off restraint, but blessed is he who keeps the law. Proverbs 29:18 ESV

> Where there is no vision, the people perish: but he that keepeth the law, happy is he. Proverbs 29:18 KJV

It's such a reminder to me to have a vision in mind of WHAT success looks like and then take steps towards obtaining that success.

Jesus, I need to think about what success really looks like inside this calling of homeschool mom. What is important? What should I be aiming for? And once I know what success looks like, help me take steps towards obtaining that success. Come alongside me and guide me in this. You are wise. You have the answers and the strength I need. Help me. In Your name I pray, Amen.

Further Reading: Proverbs 29:17-21

138

The Most Important Lesson for Our Children
Ashley Moore

When thinking of schooling my children at home the overwhelm sets in quickly.

The fear the entirety of their education rests on my ill-equipped shoulders. The fear of judgment from other moms who love to craft with their kids when I barely let them get the crayons out. Will my parents, who chose to send us to public school, support my decision? As I reign these chaotic thoughts into submission I ask myself this pointed question. What is it I want my kids to have learned when they fly the coop? I go to my hope source, the Word of God, and remind myself of the following truth:

"If I could speak in the tongues of men and of angels, but have not love, I am a noisy gong or a clanging cymbal." 1 Corinthians 13:1 ESV

Mama, will it truly matter our kids learned how to read at age four or age seven? Will it be eternally important that we let them learn on the living room floor or at a designated classroom in your home?

Will they remember they got to do lots of crafts or will they remember being surrounded by family?

What's more important, what people think about homeschool or being obedient to Christ? Scripture provides our minds with the peace we need for this type of endless worrying.

Our children can have an abundance of brilliant knowledge when they leave our homes. They can speak foreign languages with poise and precision. They can do math problems blind-folded if that's what we decide to invest in them. But according to the unfailing word of God, if they are bankrupt of love their lives will be meaningless. So today when your thoughts begin that spiral of endless comparisons and questioning if you're doing enough, ask yourself this. Have I modeled love to my children today?

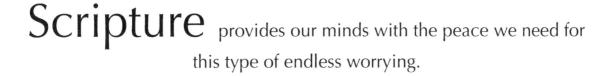

Scripture provides our minds with the peace we need for this type of endless worrying.

Dear Lord, thank you that you have given me everything I need to make my worrisome mind obedient to truth. Thank you for this timeless reminder. When the world is noisy about my child's education the most important thing they can know is how to love. Lord let that motivate me today to love them well. Let that guide all of today's activities and interactions. Let them leave this home and be known by their great love for you and for your people. In Jesus' name, Amen.

Further Reading: 1 Corinthians 13

When No One Claps For You
Trudie Schar

Every day we notice all the little things our people do. We encourage our spouses. We cheer for our little people. Every day we hope that what we do has deep and lasting meaning to those we love.

We notice.

We clap.

We cheer.

Yet as moms, what about us? Do we still need a word of encouragement? Do we need someone to clap for us?

Being a mom is hard work

It's tempting to lose hope that what we do is of any significance. We make it on time to appointments. We carry in all four library bags. We pay the late fees. We call the insurance company. We pay the bills. We pack the lunches. We make supper, well, if cereal is considered supper; we made it. We pick up the milk. We pick up the coats off the floor, again. And as we tuck the kids into bed with kisses and go out to the finally quiet kitchen, does anyone notice?

Maybe our children said a thank you throughout the day…maybe not.

Maybe our husbands notice the house was picked up…maybe he had a rough day and didn't notice.

Maybe a parent stopped in and gave us a compliment…maybe we don't have parents close.

There just might be a chance that no one noticed and no one clapped for us moms today. Let's face it…it just might happen.

I'm just going to say it out loud… I NEED someone to notice me.

I need someone to cheer me on! Yet many times, clapping just doesn't come.

When I need encouragement, I find myself with one of these two reactions…

- I go to others and search for their attention.
- I go to God for His Truth.

You know which one is the right place to go searching don't you? It is sure not others. Friend, go to God. At the end of a long day and no one seems to have noticed that you have done anything, go to God… What does He say about you? Is He clapping?

He sees everything you do. He is there to cheer you on. I promise, He has His eye on you.

How precious to me are your thoughts, O God! How vast is the sum of them!
Psalm 139:17 ESV

How precious also are thy thoughts unto me, O God! how great is the sum of them!
Psalm 139:17 KJV

Jesus, sometimes I just want someone to notice all the work I do. Sometimes I just want someone to clap for me. Someone to say "good job". Someone to see me. I know that You see everything I do. I praise You for that. I wonder — what do you say about me? Fill me with Your Spirit. In Jesus' name, Amen.

Further Reading: Psalm 139

Celebrate
Jodie Wolfe

Dear Homeschool mama,

You made it through the year! Celebrate!

Have you ever noticed how often in scripture the Israelites celebrated? I think we get so caught up with things, we forget to take time to commemorate various occasions - whether they are big or small things in our lives.

I have two grown sons. They are three years apart. For a time when they were young, they shared a bedroom. They slept in a set of bunk beds. One day, I was putting fresh sheets on the bottom bunk. My five-year-old son at the time crawled up on the top bed (not his) and leaned over to watch me. I cautioned him to get back from the edge, and then I went back to the task of putting the fitted sheet on the bed when I heard a thump.

My son had slipped off and landed on his side on the floor. I won't go into all the details but after a doctor visit and being sent immediately to the emergency room, we learned he had fractured his spleen. Because of the severity of the injury, he had a life-flight via helicopter to a bigger hospital. When we watched the helicopter take off, we had no way of knowing if we would see our son again on this earth. Despite the unknown, we had a sense of peace that God was in control.

Our son spent most of a week in intensive care, needed a blood transfusion, and eventually came home from the hospital with strict orders of a month of rest. He was only allowed to get up to walk to the bathroom and then back to bed. A difficult task for an active, energetic five-year-old.

Throughout that time, many people were praying. From all over the world. People we didn't even know. At the end of his bed rest, he had a doctor visit. It was there we saw the before and after scans of his spleen. What had been completely obliterated into many, many pieces, God completely restored to a whole, healthy spleen.

To celebrate, we decided to have a 'Praise God' party afterward. We celebrated the miracle God had performed in our son. We had an open house, inviting many who had prayed for our son. He requested his favorite foods - hot dogs and macaroni and cheese, which became the favorite birthday meal he asked for all of his nineteen years of living at home.

If my son's spleen had been removed, he would've been on antibiotics the rest of his life. This would have prevented him from his current employment.

So celebrate, Mama. Celebrate all the ups and downs from your homeschool year. Thank God that with all you faced, He brought you through each hurdle.

And David and all the house of Israel were celebrating before the Lord, with songs and lyres and harps and tambourines and castanets and cymbals. 2 Samuel 6:5 ESV

Thank You, Lord for the end of a school year. Thank You for Your provisions throughout the year. Help me to learn to celebrate the big and little things in my life. Help me to look for ways I can celebrate You and Your many blessings. In Jesus' name, Amen.

Further Reading: Ecclesiastes 3:1-8

Guest Authors

Charlotte-Anne B. Allen:

I am a self-employed speech-language pathologist in private practice, approaching 34 years of service. The years we homeschooled our daughter, all the way through, were both challenging and special. We could not have done so without the support and contribution of all my family and I would not trade those years for anything. You can visit me at www.forjustaweed.com

A Variety of Gifts — 9

To-Do's and Schedules, Oh My! — 77

Nancy Beach:

Nancy Beach received her Bachelor of Science in Bible, with honors, and is working on a Master of Arts in counseling. She has been married for 27 years and has two grown children. Nancy enjoys reading, sunsets, and sand in her toes. You can find her at www.filledtoempty.com.

Clean Kitchens are Overrated — 7

Good Enough — 82

Sue Bione:

I am a mother of 4, trauma therapist, and faithful follower of God.

Humble in Anxious Times — 29

Alone Alone — 94

Phyllis Keith Boles:

Phyllis has completed her twenty-year homeschooling journey. She has enjoyed teaching her three adult children. Her reward is to see them move into the places where God desires to meet them.

Patiently Listening — 122

Cindy Coppa:

Cindy Coppa is a past homeschooling mom, gardener, and landscape designer who is passionate about connecting people to nature and their Creator, especially children. She is a certified designer of natural play spaces and outdoor learning environments. Cindy writes from her home in New Jersey and currently has two books in progress. You can find her at www.creationcomforts.com — A respite of natural beauty for moms with insights for natural play and learning.

Natural Play and God's Voice — 19

Developing Deep Roots — 89

Chantal Dube

Chantal Dube is a professional harpist and homeschool mom of two. Seven years ago she chose to homeschool as a lifestyle choice. It helps her balance a career in performing while still taking time to be with her children. You can find her on YouTube, IG @littleharpist or follow her spiritual journey at intheclay.co

Accept not Expect — 52

Karen Geiser:

Karen Geiser, along with her husband and 5 free range children live on a family farm in Ohio. They have been homeschooling 20+ years and are grateful to be stewards of a beautiful piece of God's Creation.

Exploring Creation — 119

In the Garden — 133

Debbie Gibson

Debbie and her husband, Dan, have been married for 35 years, and have 9 children, ranging in age from 33 to 16. All of the children have been home educated from birth. Debbie & Dan enjoy serving their family, their church family, and the homeschool community together.

Safe in the Storm — 27

He is Our Refuge — 112

Jessica Heinlen

I'm a country mama of 6 and married to my high school sweetheart for 17 years. I'm passionate about Jesus, coffee, homeschooling and quiet mornings.

You Are Called — 4

Do it With a Will — 109

Tandy Sue Hogate

Tandy is a writer, farmer's wife, and homeschool mama. She loves sharing modern applications to God's beautiful ancient wisdom. You can find her at www.ordinarylifeextraordinarygod.com or on IG and FB sharing stories on the pages of Ordinary Life Extraordinary God. Please stop by and say Hi! She loves making new friends!

Build Your Wall — 17

Self Care, It's Not What You Think — 49

Stop, Mama, And Look Them In The Eyes — 102

We Lead Gently Because He Gently Leads — 136

Kira Jahn

Kira is a homeschooling mom of four young boys. While she believes academics are important, the state of her children's hearts takes priority in their day to day. She desires to encourage families to take discipleship of their children seriously by providing resources through her Instagram platform @alongsidethem.

Homeschooling is Sanctification — 67

Tecia Janes

Tecia Janes is an author, speaker and founder of Choosing Him Ministries. CHM is a women's ministry that connects women to Jesus, God's Word and to each other. It is also a place for women to submit their blogs to encourage women in their daily walk. You can find out more about this ministry at choosinghimministries.org

Grace, Grace, God's Grace — 57

Cheryl Kischuk

Cheryl Kischuk is a Christian, wife, homeschool mom to three children, and founder of the Epiphanies365 ministry. Her perspective is that any experience in life can be spun as a positive educational adventure. She loves to encourage parents that they are valuable and, when called, are tremendously equipped and capable.

How do You Best Connect With God? — 37

What is Your Identity? — 79

Angel Lambert

I have been a Christ follower pretty much my entire life and a writer for almost as long. Short stories are fun, but poetry is my passion. My husband and I have four sons and believe homeschooling is the best parental freedom in this country, and I am here to encourage that you can do it, too.

The Father Who Forgives the Daughter Who Forgets — 62

Roots of Hurt and Blame — 131

Jodi Leman

I am a child of God, wife and mother of 4 with one on the way. We live in IL while not on the mission field in PNG where my husband is a helicopter pilot.

Do Not Worry — 12

Good Works —92

Sarah Lindsay

I am a follower of Jesus Christ, wife, and mother to 4 children. I love studying the Word of God, reading books, and spending time with my family.

Checed" — 69

Tara Maxheimer

A happy homeschooling mama to 6 sweet blessings. Teaching for 10 years, wife for 15 years, Jesus follower for 32 years.

Who Am I? — 32

Too Busy to not Make Time — 87

Ashley Moore

Ashley writes on her blog authorashleymoore.com and her IG @ashleymoorexo to illuminate the truth that salvation is only the beginning of a beautiful journey with the Lord. At the core of everything she does is a message to encourage and equip believers to abide, obey and make an impact for the Kingdom of God. In addition to this, Ashley is a wife to Colby Moore and mama to her three precious children Cypress, Sparrow & Jovee.

Reminder for the Mama Who Yelled Today — 59

The Most Important Lesson for Our Children — 138

Brittney Morris

Brittney Morris, is a Jesus lover, wife, and mama of 3, has homeschooled for 4 years. She is the Associate Director of Women's Ministry at Grace Fellowship Church Shrewsbury in PA. Find her blog at wordfilledwoman.wordpress.com or follow her on Instagram @brittneymorrisauthor.

Come to the Table — 14

1,000 Questions — 74

It's Not About Curriculum — 117

Melody Plessinger

I am a mom of 4. Humbly homeschooling with lots of grace with the help of my Heavenly Father.

Unless Jesus — 39

When It Isn't July Anymore — 72

Danielle Hope Poorman

Danielle is a former homeschool teacher and now homeschooling mom of two children. She writes at DanielleHope.com where she encourages and renews mothers to cultivate calmness so they can experience joy in motherhood.

Darcy Schock

Darcy lives in central Illinois with her husband and three daughters. She loves quiet days of reading, writing, and a lot of coffee. You can find more of her writings at hellojesusco.com.

Barb Schwind

Barb Schwind is from central Illinois. She has taught students with disabilities in the public schools for over 30 years. She and her husband, Dave, love Jesus, working with young people, hiking and walking, and helping their 4 young grandchildren learn.

Stephanie H. Short

Stephanie is a faith-inpsired homeschool mom who loves to write in her spare time. She is also heavily involved in her local homeschool cooperative and loves working with children and their families.

Tabatha Slater

Tabatha is first and foremost a daughter of the King. She has been happily married to her husband Matthew for over 25 years. Eight beautiful blessings call her mom. Tabatha has been homeschooling for over twenty years.

Friends — 47

The Journey — 124

Cynthia Stoller

I am a follower of Christ and homeschool mom with 3 graduates, 4 in school, and 2 toddlers from TN. God is faithful and good!

You and Your Kids are Unique — 24

Grace is Sufficient —104

Toni Studer

Toni Studer is a wife and mother to 4 kids (3 girls and a boy). She has been homeschooling for seven years. She has a passion for helping other homeschool moms through this exciting journey. She has a YouTube channel where she reviews curriculum and gives tips on homeschooling and being thrifty. Her channel is called Our Thrifty Homeschool.

Be Still — 22

Broken Jar — 107

Jodie Wolfe

Jodie Wolfe creates novels where hope and quirky meet. A former columnist for Home School Enrichment magazine, her articles can be found online at: Crosswalk, Christian Devotions, and Heirloom Audio. Learn more at www.jodiewolfe.com.

God and Sticky Notes —34

Can I Glorify God with My Body and Eat Chocolate Too? — 84

Lessons Caught — 99

Go to the Source that Never Runs Dry — 114

Celebrate — 140

Author

Trudie Schar: Trudie is married to her high school sweetheart, Ethan. She's called mama by four girls whom she homeschools. She is an introvert who found a real relationship with Jesus when He called her to homeschool and travel a path of forgiveness. Trudie writes and speaks about filling up on Jesus so we freely pour out to serve our people. She loves gathering women to encourage each other through planning events like Sister Share and Homeschool Mom's Night. She also enjoys equipping others to use their gifts through her role as the Study Manager at Hello Jesus Co and as Community Director at Teach Them Diligently 365. Some of her favorite things are quiet moments with God, hanging out with her family, and drinking hot cocoa with friends.

Trudie's podcast and Instagram are both titled Learning Little Lessons. Visit her website at learninglittlelessons.com.

Made in the USA
Columbia, SC
07 May 2021